FUTURE FARM BLUEPRINT

Plan your sustainability journey with clarity and confidence

BY LIZ OTTO

First published in 2018 by Grammar Factory

© Liz Otto 2018

The moral rights of the author have been asserted

All enquiries should be made to the author.

Printed in Australia by McPherson's Printing Group
Text design by Charlotte Gelin Design
Cover design by Designerbility
Editing by Grammar Factory

A catalogue record for this
book is available from the
National Library of Australia

Disclaimer

The material in this publication is of the nature of general comment only, and does
not represent professional advice. It is not intended to provide specific guidance for
particular circumstances and it should not be relied on as the basis for any decision
to take action or not take action on any matter which it covers. Readers should obtain
professional advice where appropriate, before making any such decision. To the
maximum extent permitted by law, the author and publisher disclaim all responsibility
and liability to any person, arising directly or indirectly from any person taking or not
taking action based on the information in this publication.

What others are saying

'*Future Farm Blueprint is a very useful and needed resource. The book brings the fullness and complexity of primary production to the table and to people's awareness, and then has the ability to break that into bite-sized chunks that fit together logically.*'

Nikki Thompson, Coach, Inner Circle Work and Director, Echo Hills Farming Company and Soil2Soul.

'*Having had the chance to read this book in draft, I know you are in for a treat! If you are interested in practical and outcome-focused planning for your farming business, this is the book for you. It is equally as useful for anyone working with family in any business. Easy to read, packed with ideas and great questions, this book will help you move your business and, importantly, your people forward.*'

Julia Telford, Director, Engage and Create Consulting.

'*Natural Resource Management is an integral part of the management of successful modern agricultural businesses. Future Farm Blueprint provides a process to guide you through the development of a comprehensive plan for your business. Importantly, the process ensures all necessary people are involved and considers many aspects of farm management beyond NRM over short, medium and long-term timeframes.*'

Ian McLean, Director, Bush Agribusiness Pty Ltd.

Acknowledgements

Thank you to my family and friends who have supported my leaps of faith, first in starting a business and now as an author.

Writing a book has been an opportunity to reflect on the experiences, insights and accomplishments gained over many years. I am deeply grateful for my special mentors and colleagues for their encouragement.

To all my clients, your trust in me is appreciated. It is such a pleasure to be part of your journey and to see the return for your efforts towards your goals.

There is great support available for people like me who are looking to do more, achieve more and contribute more. Thank you to the Dent crew and my publishing team for the guidance and accountability. I am doing exactly what I am meant to.

Contents

FARM LOGIC MAP FIGURES

Introduction

Do you have a clear vision of what you want your farm to look like in, say, twenty years' time? Do you understand the best way to manage your land, the condition of resources and profitability for the long term? Can you describe what being a sustainable farmer or land custodian means to you, and how connected you are to the broader landscape, community and economy?

Farmers who aspire to be sustainable think deeply about what it means to them and what it looks like for their farm. They have a vision for a healthy and thriving environment, a robust and integrated production system, a profitable and accomplished business, and a secure and supportive lifestyle. They feel a profound sense of connection to their land, its past and future, and its place in the landscape. They feel responsibility for the actions they take and for those taken before them, and they strive to restore the natural balance and improve resilience.

A sustainable farming business is about prioritising production and natural systems, environmental and social stewardship, wellbeing and lifestyle, and community connectedness. Sustainability planning involves:

- A deep understanding of natural systems and production cycles and cause-and-effect relationships;
- Acknowledging micro, paddock, property and landscape processes;
- Integrating economic and social drivers; and
- Assessment and management of threatening processes and risks.

However, farmers often find it difficult to capture current operations and future aspirations in a way that is easy, logical and communicable. Industry programs provide a framework for standard practice but lack integration and recognition of mixed farming enterprises or land use. The planning and reporting are linear and do not take into account the complexities of the natural and operating systems and business situation. Not being able to demonstrate the linkages across operations leads to duplication in reporting to meet external purposes. Specialist consulting groups may offer broader frameworks, but they are often associated with a particular school of thought or production system.

Without a planning framework that supports integration and a change management process over time, further problems arise. Without a plan in place, it is difficult for farmers to communicate their intentions to others, whether they be the people on their team, service providers or potential partners. The goals may not be well defined and, therefore, decisions are less focused on the future state and become more bogged down in day-to-day operations. The theory of change is unsubstantiated and carried out by trial and error, without purposeful monitoring data or the ability to query it effectively.

Success still happens. It is the determination, experience and attitude of these farmers that provide scope for positive change. But it can be an inefficient and ineffective process, with much effort spent overcoming barriers and convincing others.

The lack of planning results in one or more of the following issues:

- Farmers aren't clear about what they want to achieve and why it is important to them.

- They don't fully understand their situation.

- They are uncertain whether they have the capability to implement priority actions.

- They can't substantiate the success of their approach.

Have you thought about what sustainability means to you? Do you know how the rest of the team feels about it? Have you identified the current barriers that are stopping you from attaining your desired future?

Maybe your future desires are clear. Or, potentially, just asking these questions may result in an overwhelming feeling of uncertainty and lack of direction. Either way, you might be stuck about what to do or how to go about it. It is easy to get caught up in operational matters with no clear purpose or to start projects without long-term plans in place. Your team might be feeling the same, resulting in poor performance or a lack of purpose. These problems can manifest over time or hit with sudden overwhelm.

If this is you, then your next question will likely be: What can I do about it? Well, you have already taken the first step. This book is designed to help you navigate the decision-making process in order to set and achieve longer-term sustainability goals.

Planning is my passion

I am not a farmer, but I am passionate about agriculture and even more passionate about planning for sustainability.

For many years I worked with Landcare, catchment and regional groups on projects such as riparian fencing, weed and pest management, riverine health assessments, water use efficiency, salinity and land type fencing, to mention a few. I supported cotton farmers implementing the industry accreditation program and managed a number of local government programs.

I have been involved in all levels of planning: working with landholders at the property and neighbourhood scale to prepare natural resource management plans; supporting local government weed and pest planning; and preparing catchment and regional natural resource management plans and programs.

I started consulting in 2012 so I could help farmers, supporting organisations and agri-businesses overcome the barriers to attaining sustainability goals, by specialising in planning and grant writing. As a consultant, I have supported over 200 landholders and 50 businesses and organisations.

From my experience and training, I have designed a four-stage methodology that encompasses different aspects of farming, enabling farmers to effectively plan and achieve future sustainability goals. I work with farmers to quickly and competently identify the source of their issues and help them find their own clarity, capacity and confidence in order to move forward.

The blueprint methodology is not a new concept. Each component, on its own, you may already be familiar with. But what I have found, after nearly twenty years in the agricultural industry, is the lack of an overarching approach that works with people beyond the paddock and considers the entirety of their situation, business and goals. A one-size-fits-all approach to management does not take into account the things influencing each unique situation. Some of those things are in the control of management; some are not. It is knowing the difference between what can be controlled and what can't, and how to address each situation, that is key to future success.

I hope that by sharing my understanding of and experiences in strategic farm planning and delivery, I can help you navigate the entirety of your situation and gain the confidence to manage change towards your vision of sustainability.

Future Farm Blueprint user guide

This book is a guide to helping farmers (landholders, property owners, managers, corporate entities, etc.) and their team (family, partners, staff, consultants, service providers, etc.) plan and achieve sustainability goals with clarity and confidence. I will walk you through:

- The planning process via four key stages;
- How to involve your team; and
- How to put together the right plans for your farming business.

With a good process in place, any complexity of issues across any scale can be broken down into its parts and managed effectively.

The four parts to this book align with the four key planning phases:

1. **Clarity** – Become clear about what is important to you and your team, what you want to achieve and why. This is documented in a strategic plan.

2. **Knowledge** – Explore the current state of the assets and how you see those assets in the future. A management plan will set specific goals and strategies.

3. **Capability** – Plan deliverable actions, including annual action and project plans.

4. **Confidence** – Keep confidently on the right tracks by collecting evidence that you are achieving the desired goals with a Monitoring, Evaluation, Reporting and Improvement (MERI) Plan.

The methodology presented in this book shows how to prepare a Future Farm Blueprint in a straightforward, easy-to-follow way. Each of the four parts will:

- Introduce why the step is important, who needs to be involved and the purpose of the plan;
- Discuss the methodology and provide personal examples (italics text);
- Provide practical exercises and steps to work through with your team; and
- Demonstrate how to write a Strategic, Management, Action and MERI Plan.

Throughout the book, we visit a simple case study designed to bring parallels to some of the situations you may be faced with. The case study characters are fictional; however, all the circumstances presented are real-life experiences I have encountered over years.

The book teaches a planning process to organise your thoughts and to guide your decision-making. By understanding the full process, you will be well placed to readily identify your current challenges and their root causes.

A range of resources are available from the PLAN FOR NRM website (www.plannfornrm.com.au), along with links to other useful resources, to help you over the course of your planning. These include tips, templates, guides and tools. The site is updated regularly, so be sure to check in and see what has been added. If there are gaps in resources that would be helpful to your situation, let me know and I will see if it is something I already have or can prepare for you.

Case Study – Paige Pastoral Pty Ltd

The Paige Family (Mark and Jane, Nigel and Mary)

Let me introduce you to the Paige family. Mark and Jane Paige are in business with their son Nigel and his wife, Mary. Paige Pastoral Pty Ltd is a cattle grazing enterprise located on the Western Darling Downs, Queensland. The business manages three properties covering 8,500 hectares.

Mark and Jane are thinking about scaling back and handing the responsibility of the farms to Nigel and Mary. Trying to avoid the issues they experienced in the handover of the original family farm from Mark's parents, the family recently put in place a succession plan. This process has brought to front-of mind-the condition in which they want to leave the farms, not only for Nigel and his family, but also for future generations.

The Paige family has adopted a rotational grazing system which is focused on increasing groundcover and biodiversity, and improving soil health and animal performance. They have progressively converted old cultivation to improved pastures. The business is profitable. The family is supported by a permanent farm manager on one of the properties, Bill Long who is a valued member of the team. The properties are in better condition now than when they were acquired.

Overall, the Paige family seems to have found their sweet spot for enhancing production, protecting the environment, making money, enjoying life and serving their community. But there remain many pressures on the farm that impact on production and cause stress. The family has engaged in various courses and industry programs, but felt they were not on top of all the issues. Wanting to be proactive, the family decided that a more integrated and longer-term approach was needed.

As we work through the book, we will visit the Paige family to see how the methodology applies to their situation. For the full case study, including a copy of their Plans and Farm Logic Maps, visit www.planfornrm.com.au. You will also find real case studies of farming teams and their experiences preparing their Future Farm Blueprint.

PART 1

CLARITY

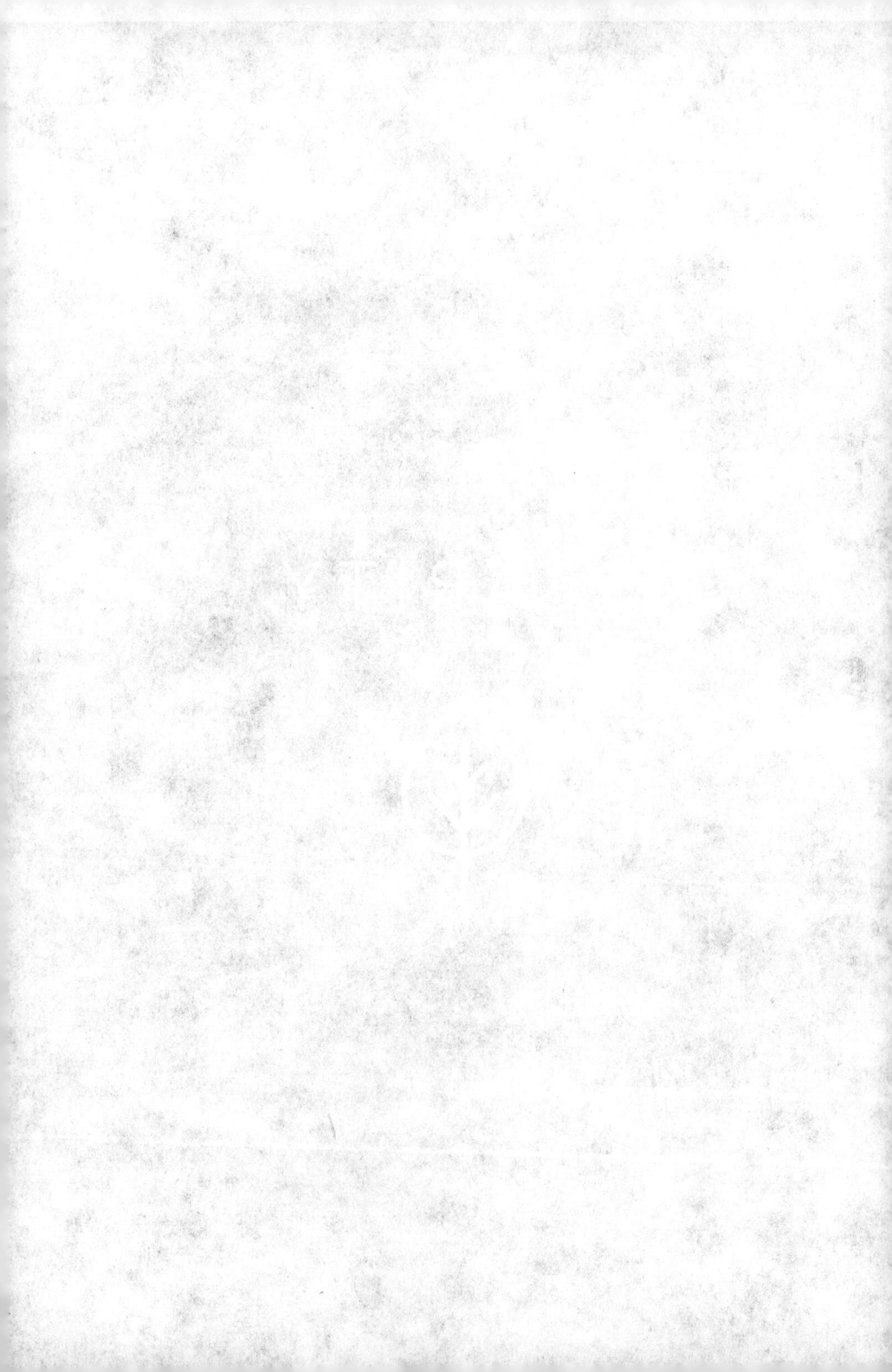

CHAPTER 1

A Strategic Blueprint for Your Future Farm

Farming is more than just a job or business. It is about passion, lifestyle and heritage. Farming is also a big commitment. Whether your farm is new to you, has been in the family for generations, or is leased or managed, it is no doubt important to you. Before setting goals and actions, it is helpful to step back and think about what your farm and being a farmer mean to you. Those thoughts will impact on how you would describe your ideal situation in the future.

What does the future look like?

What is it about this future that is important to you?

Who will share the journey with you?

What is driving you to make a change?

Those farming businesses attaining their sustainability goals are clear about what they want to achieve and why it is important to them.

The first part of this book is dedicated to achieving clarity about the future of your business through a strategic planning process, documented in a strategic plan. This involves bringing members of the team together to actively participate in the development of a shared vision and underpinning values, and collectively describing the ideal future. A strategic plan simply documents the decisions of the team. This becomes a point of reference that guides all future decisions.

The value of strategic planning is sometimes not seen until you have been through the process. It can be hard to pinpoint current problems, and a lack of leadership, direction or clear decision-making can leave teams simply reacting to issues as they arise. This can result in a narrow focus on day-to-day operations and chasing short-term gains to stay afloat. As with any business team, losing sight of the key goals and purposes can be detrimental to making good decisions for the future and keeping the business on track.

If you assume that you know what family members, business partners or staff want, they may become disengaged. The simple process of asking them questions about their aspirations and what is important to them can change the dynamics of relationships and even address feelings of worth. By being proactive on things important to them, the team can enjoy a positive experience and avoid a reactionary approach leading to decisions being made that are not supported or valued.

The chapters in part one will:

- Discuss why strategic planning is important;

- Demonstrate how to work with the team through a strategic planning process; and

- Show how key elements of the plan document may be presented.

Why do you need a strategic plan?

A STRATEGIC PLAN basically describes what your future farm looks like and what it means to the team and business. It is designed to provide scope for a call to action on matters that are important. Operational decisions should align with the strategic plan.

How a strategic plan is developed is just as critical as the plan itself. Strategic planning will bring together the people who share your goal for the business. It will bring to the surface the shared values as well as the differences across the team, and provide an opportunity to agree on what is important and what you collectively want to achieve.

Strategic planning will also help determine what is outside the scope of the business and what is unrealistic to address. Documenting your decisions about the intentions of the business will make priorities clear for the team and other stakeholders. The plan becomes a point of agreement and validation when it comes to future actions.

The absence of a strategic plan often results in a lack of clarity and agreement about what the business hopes to achieve and why. A robust decision-making process brings about collective agreement, so a lack of this can lead to frustration, with expectations about what the team intends to achieve differing across members. This chapter will help you to avoid potential problems by having everyone on the same page.

I recently had the pleasure of working with a farming team to prepare a strategic plan for their business. They are forward thinkers with deep aspirations for long-term healthy production systems that nurture their environment, people and community. The three families were already close and working well together. However, by trying to communicate with everyone on the team, decision-making would often be slow and ad hoc. Team members didn't know what information and consultation they needed until they came to the point of making a decision. This was because they didn't have a common understanding of business values and goals.

Therefore, the process of sharing their values and ambitions and coming to an agreed position was liberating for the team. Each person felt understood and articulated their collective purpose with intent and clarity. Big decisions they were struggling with prior to this process are now guided by an agreed reference point. Each member of the team has the confidence to act based on values, principles and goals that give clear direction about what is in, and what is out. The process affirmed their own relationships and desires for the business and validated their 'gut feel' about the type of people and businesses they wanted to work with in pursuit of their goals.

By walking through a strategic planning process, you can articulate and reconnect with your aspirations and the aspirations of the team to find a renewed sense of energy and focus. This, in itself, makes the plan self-fulfilling.

A strategic plan should be focused on what is important and why. Other types of planning will focus on how to overcome the issues and the actions required to achieve the desired goals. But the 'why' must be established first. This relates to the shared values of the people involved and is covered in more detail in the next chapter. For now, consider the benefits of having an agreed plan to guide the future of your farming business.

ACTION: WORK WITH YOUR TEAM

Have a discussion with your team about the benefits of having an agreed strategic plan. This discussion will inform the purpose of the plan.

What is the purpose of your strategic plan?

Strategic planning aims to develop a shared vision with the team. It is designed to bring clarity to the intentions and direction of the business – what the business aims to achieve and why it is important.

A strategic plan can be used internally in different ways, such as:

- Communicating the overarching mission, values, goals and commitments of the business.

- Guiding further planning and actions to bring about improvement to the current situation.

- Validating whether actions have achieved the intended goals.

- Directing how the change process is managed.

A strategic plan can be a powerful document that strengthens the pursuit of the business. It allows the team to consistently and confidently communicate with external parties. This might be in the process of talking with suppliers, agents or contractors, attending industry meetings, establishing partnerships, applying for funding, employing new staff, responding to consultation processes, demonstrating social responsibility, and advocacy.

Strategic plans can sometimes be viewed as big-picture, blue-sky fluff, which nobody reads anyway. And there are situations where this perception is understandable. If you have heard such negative comments, it might be because there have been past experiences of poor strategic planning. The people affected may not have been directly involved in the plan development, or the plan itself did not reflect what was discussed and agreed.

A robust strategic planning process will achieve a high level of understanding and appreciation across the team; this will provide a foundation for more-collaborative decision-making. The team will feel connected to the overall vision of the business and will contribute positively to its pursuits and activities.

It is important that your team understands why and how a strategic planning process and plan will help them achieve the business goals. Documenting the purpose of the plan and its intended use is the first section of the strategic plan.

ACTION: WORK WITH YOUR TEAM

Have a discussion with your team about how a strategic plan may be used.

Who will be involved?

It is helpful to identify who will be involved in developing the plan. This is because a strategic plan not only informs business decisions, but also the values and even the culture of the business.

What level of involvement will different people in your business need to have to create meaningful direction and ownership?

For a family farming business, the plan may involve the owners, family members, farm manager and, if appropriate, the permanent staff. The approach is flexible and can take into account the current situation as well as helping you make decisions regarding succession or as different arrangements come into play.

For larger, corporate farms, the business owners and management team may be largely responsible for the strategic plan. However, there should be opportunities for staff to have input. This may be achieved through having representatives at management meetings and team meetings, and by conducting surveys and discussions with individuals. One of the key questions is: What is it about this farm that makes you want to work here and not somewhere else? This reflects the values and culture of the organisation.

Not identifying and appropriately engaging the right people from the start can impact the adoption and delivery of the plan. Remember, the process of plan development is usually more important than the plan itself. Why? People need to feel they are being heard on issues important to them, they want to participate in and understand the decision-making, and they want to engage in a robust process in order to connect with and accept the final decision. This is true for individuals and for whole industry groups. People do not like things done to or for them, regardless of whether the final plan aligns with their position.

ACTION: WORK WITH YOUR TEAM

Identify the target audiences and roles in relation to the strategic plan.

- Who has ownership of the plan?
- Who has an interest in the plan?
- What level of engagement is appropriate for each person?
- Who is responsible for overseeing the delivery of the plan?

Clearly communicate with each audience their intended role and the nature of their participation in the development of the strategic plan.

ACTION: WRITE YOUR STRATEGIC PLAN

Heading: Purpose of the Plan
In the opening section of your business strategic plan, describe what the plan will document and how the plan will be used.

Heading: Who it is for
Provide a brief description of the key people involved and their connection
to the plan.

Heading: Stakeholders
Provide a brief description of interested and affected parties.

Heading: About us
This is a good place to provide an outline of the business, including a brief
history of its achievements, functions and hopes for the future. This is usually
not documented elsewhere, so it provides a handy reference.

CHAPTER 2

What is Important and Why?

Unless you are on your own, there will be other people connected to the business who will have personal reasons why they are involved with the business and what they hope to personally gain from that involvement. To reach a collective decision about business goals, it is helpful to acknowledge and understand the motivating factors for each person.

Each member of the team will have personal connections to the farm, and different values and aspirations. The question of what those values are and how the farm should be managed for the benefit of individuals and the business as a whole is the source of much conflict, particularly for family farms. It can also be a point of solidarity and connection when deeply shared.

Acknowledging this, it is worth exploring the underlying reasons that have brought the team together, identifying what unites them and what might potentially divide them. Some business managers become so focused on delivering the business purpose that they forget why people have chosen to be there in the first place. If personal relevance to the goal gets lost, people start to feel they are contributing more than they are getting in return. Decisions will be better supported if personal connections are recognised.

Clarity starts with me, then we. Individuals and the business as a whole benefit from clarity about what is driving people to participate in the first place. Finding common ground and shared purpose then becomes much easier.

The personal WHY

Most people have deep personal reasons for being where they are, but also greater aspirations for where they want to be. Ask yourself these questions and then ask the team to share their responses.

> **What are your aspirations for the farm?**
>
> **Where do you see your lifestyle, business or situation in ten years' time?**
>
> **What is important about the work you do and how you live your life?**
>
> **Why are you here and not doing something else?**

Behind decisions and aspirations are values. These are the beliefs, traits or qualities that contribute to an individual's moral compass. Values relate to what people desire in life and include deep personal priorities like friendship, respect, equality, security, peace, comfort, ambition, honesty, responsibility, intellect, logic, and so on.

Individuals are invited to name their values, i.e. what is important to them. These can then be grouped, and a list of CORE VALUES or a value statement can be generated that reflects the overall sentiments of the team. This is a process that needs to be facilitated, and it's hard to predict how the discussion will flow and requires a certain amount of intuition and gut feeling.

Identifying and naming values, such as integrity, respect and responsibility, will help the team be more proactive and live by these agreed expectations. It makes using intuition more acceptable, for example, when questioning why and how you do business with others. It is helpful to identify individuals and organisations who share or do not share your core values so that conflict can be addressed.

Having identified the team values and concerns, the next step is to talk about the benefits of being part of the farm business.

What do you enjoy about being part of this farm team?

Often, people will enjoy the support of working with like-minded people, sharing experiences and learning from each other. The capacity of a team is more than just the combined skills and knowledge of its individuals; it is augmented by their understanding, passion, unique experiences, and networks established over time. This means that one plus one becomes more than two.

If people cannot personally connect with the direction of the business, they will be critical of decisions and actions, have poor experiences and become disengaged. A business does not need to cater for every individual, but every individual needs to be clear about their connection with the business.

When individuals are clear about why they want to be involved, what they will get out of it and what they will contribute, it gives the overall team clarity. Having each individual consider and articulate their values, experiences and expected benefits will prepare them for the endeavours of the business. It will also help the team to quickly and effectively generate shared connections and reach agreement on priority issues and actions.

ACTION: WORK WITH YOUR TEAM

With your team, consider:

- What are your core values and what is important to you? Why?
- What do you hope to gain from being involved with the business?
- What do you have to offer that would benefit the team?

Writing a vision

A VISION is a single statement that describes the overall direction of the business and its purpose. A vision acts as an anchor, ensuring that all decisions and actions directly link to, support and implement the intention of the business. The process of preparing a vision allows for discussion and agreement about what the team wants to achieve.

A vision statement needs to be short, specific to your business, simple and ambitious, and it needs to align with the team's values. Writing a vision for a newly formed business may rely heavily on the why and values sessions to build a common appreciation of what it is the team wishes to pursue. Setting or reviewing a vision is a useful exercise to bring together everyone's thoughts and ambitions into a concise focus point.

The first step is to think about what the business does, produces or delivers. What is the outcome from these activities? For example, Paige Pastoral produces quality beef using regenerative and contemporary welfare practices. The outcome is sustainably and ethically produced, nutritious and tasty food.

The second step is to define what your business does that is unique or different from what others are doing, or how it fills a gap. What makes your business special? Paige Pastoral specialises in certified 100% organic grass-fed premium beef.

The third step is to quantify the end point. This might describe a location, an audience or a target. Paige Pastoral targets profitable local premium organic markets.

The fourth step is making the vision relatable. A highly refined statement will lack meaning if there is no human connection. What mental image do you have of the desired situation? For Paige Pastoral, it is running a family-oriented business to feed families in their community.

In summary, the vision should describe what you do, how you do it and the result, with a clear and relatable image. Having a vision allows the team to simply and easily communicate their intention to others. The vision is written as a collection of positive statements in the present tense.

Paige Pastoral is a profitable family business producing delicious premium organic grass-fed beef that is healthy for local families and the environment.

ACTION: WORK WITH YOUR TEAM

To create a vision statement, ask the following questions and collate the responses:

- What does the business do? What are the outcomes?
- What is special about your business?
- What is the end goal?

Summarise the answers in an overarching statement, making sure the image is relatable.

ACTION: WRITE YOUR STRATEGIC PLAN

Heading: Our why
List or describe the core values of the business and group into key areas if relevant.

Heading: Our vision
Simply state your vision in bold.

Creating a Farm Logic Map

A FARM LOGIC MAP is your blueprint for change. It is a mind-mapping tool that has the capacity to set future goals and create logical steps to achieve those goals. Learning to use this tool was one of the most defining moments in my career, as it brought together the whole picture instead of working in linear tables. You can zoom out for perspective or zoom in for detail, and look to the future or assess the current priorities. It organises all of the complex and connected thoughts required to make decisions with confidence.

Throughout the book, I will walk you through using the Farm Logic Map one stage at a time, using simple examples.

To get set up, you need:

- A blank wall
- Plastic tablecloths
- 3M or other adhesive spray available at stationery stores
- Tape
- A5 coloured paper and pens

Tape the sheets of plastic tablecloth to the blank wall as high as you can comfortably reach. You may need two sheets for sufficient height. Spray the plastic with the 3M adhesive spray. This makes it slightly sticky and enables you to attach the paper and move it around.

Always take a photo of every Farm Logic Map created. It is a handy reference, and the elements do not have to be professionally typed, as I have done in the book, to be effective. Keep a permanent wall in place and use it for decision-making and planning at any time.

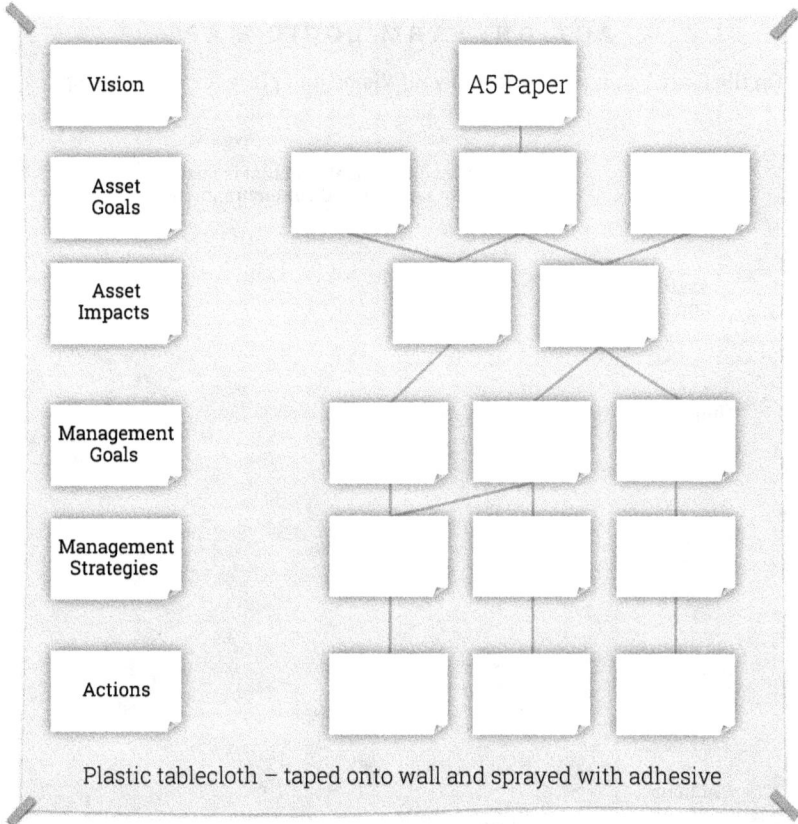

Vision

A5 Paper

Asset Goals

Asset Impacts

Management Goals

Management Strategies

Actions

Plastic tablecloth – taped onto wall and sprayed with adhesive

Farm Logic Map 1: Demonstration

ACTION: FARM LOGIC MAP

On the Farm Logic Map, write out your Vision and place it at the very top.

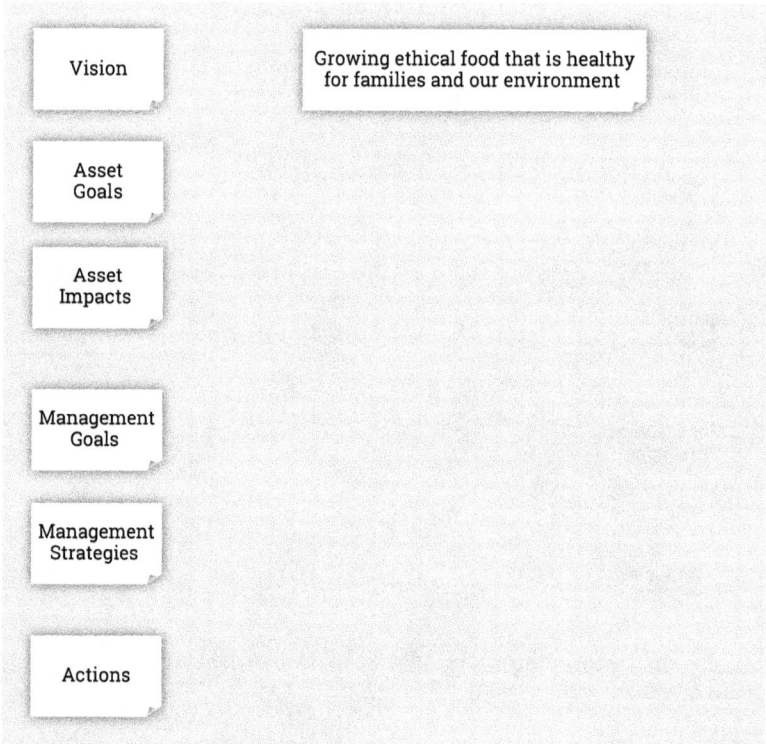

Vision	Growing ethical food that is healthy for families and our environment
Asset Goals	
Asset Impacts	
Management Goals	
Management Strategies	
Actions	

Farm Logic Map 2: Vision (Level 1) Example

CHAPTER 3

What are the Driving Factors?

There are three fundamental values attached to all assets, including those on your farm – economic, environmental and social values. In this chapter, we will explore how these fundamental values drive management decisions around sustainability outcomes. Your decisions will also be influenced by other factors such as science, politics, and community values and perspectives. The aim is to clarify the nature of these internal and external factors and how they may influence decision-making for your farm.

Understanding the three fundamental values connected with your assets will bring clarity to the issues you face. First, think about your own economic, environmental and social values when it comes to water, soil, vegetation, etc., and how they influence your management. Then, consider the same assets on your farm and how others value them: individuals; the local community; and the wider community. Values are a matter of perspective and are influenced by experience, connection and benefit to the individual.

Issues and conflict arise when management practices impact on people's values and those values impact on management practices. So, we continue to see the rise of interest groups intent on influencing the way natural resources and animals are managed. In response, industry organisations seek to resolve conflicts arising from various scientific, political or community perspectives. Understanding values clarifies the basis of those perspectives and how they can impact on your decision-making.

It is important for a strategic planning process to identify the shared environmental, economic and social values of the business. It is also important to recognise that there are values outside the business that will influence the current and future situation.

Asset values

Sustainability is about achieving a balanced fulfilment of social, environmental and economic values. This section will consider the scale, scope and extent of those values.

SOCIAL

In order to be sustainable, your business needs to consider its social values in relation to its members, including wellbeing, health, lifestyle and fulfilment, family relationships, care and security.

After taking those considerations into account, it is necessary to move on to the next level of its social values in relation to the local community. Participation in and contribution to the local community may include being of service, sharing experiences and raising awareness of broader community needs such as stable employment, access to services, health and supporting businesses. Local culture and heritage are important and underpin the identity and uniqueness of a place, bringing people together while also recognising different perspectives.

The next level of social awareness in the context of sustainability is the greater community. This is where stewardship has wide-reaching benefits, such as sharing values with others who may not be directly associated with your farm. Community awareness, education, connection and experiences become a focus, with the aim of sharing benefits with others or influencing their perceptions. This is explored further in the next section.

ENVIRONMENTAL

The term environment refers to all things natural, including the physical form, function and system, i.e. anything that lives, breathes or exists as part of a natural process. Environmental value is a matter of social perception or attitude. Connection with the environment can be passive, direct or intrinsically linked to our lifestyle, culture and income.

The extent to which we connect with environmental values may be a result of experience, education, understanding, awareness and culture. People may enjoy the environment where they live or enjoy recreational activities like swimming, fishing and bushwalking. They may appreciate birds, animals and plants or have strong cultural and historical associations with the land. They may have pursued a profession that seeks to understand the environment, manage it or utilise it for food, fibre or resource production.

Think of your own connection with the environment: locally, regionally and globally. Each member of your team will have their own personal connection with and attitude towards the natural environment and the role it has in their life.

ECONOMIC

Economic values are associated with the opportunity to generate a monetary transaction, either directly or indirectly. In agriculture, natural resources provide the foundation of income for farmers and their workers, service providers and value-adding processes. The value is the ability to generate an income and future security and provide for families and lifestyle desires, for the farmer and every other individual along the processing chain.

Economic values relate to your situation, the business, the local community and the greater community. For individuals, economic values are closely linked to the social values identified earlier that seek to provide security for self and family and to support a desired lifestyle. For community, economic value is inherent in security, availability of employment and provision of social services, as well as industry stability, infrastructure and services.

In summary, sustainability is the pursuit of the ultimate balance of social, environmental and economic values as they affect the business and community. When managed holistically, these values can be complementary. They can all be fulfilled with improved connections and control over decision-making on the farm.

ACTION: WORK WITH YOUR TEAM

Following on from the 'why' session, talk with the team and create a list of the shared broad environmental, social and economic values of the business. List the values or key points on a board as they are raised. Then go back and group them into key areas. Remove duplicates and decide if a statement about each group or simply a list is preferred by the team.

- **Social** – wellbeing, respect, integrity, teaming, cooperation, influence, etc. (internal: family/team/group; and external: local or broader community)
- **Environmental** – stewardship, care, education, awareness, understanding, etc.
- **Economic** – profitability, good governance, growth, success, etc.

Influencing factors

There are additional factors that influence the foundational economic, environmental and social values. These INFLUENCING FACTORS affect people's understanding of a situation and their ability to manage that situation. The factors can be broadly defined as scientific, social, political and economic influences unique to each situation. They may come from external sources or exist within the business or local community.

Science largely informs our understanding of the current situation, the condition of assets and trends, and the appropriateness of management practices and consequences. Science seeks to measure and understand the natural environment and the intended and unintended outcomes from its use and informs efficient and effective management decisions. Scientific information influences decision-making, whether in the paddock or on a regional or national scale where it informs policy and legislation.

Social factors may have a strong influence over how your business is perceived. Social influences might be internal to your business – such as demographics, experiences, education, and even personalities and strong leaders, etc. They might stem from circumstances where local issues have caused division in the community. Issues or circumstances that your business is trying to address might have attracted interest from the broader community or be a common issue for other communities. In these situations, public perception will be of concern. The extent to which it is representative or understanding of the local situation can have an effect on your business, how you respond, and your social licence to operate. Public perception comes back to values and how passionately and strongly certain positions are pursued.

For example, the Paige family love wildlife and have retained vegetation patches and corridors to provide a healthy habitat for it. However, improved pastures and permanent water have led to kangaroos breeding out of control. Their ability to manage groundcover and grazing pressure is hampered. These are economic and resource issues to Paige Pastoral. But choosing to manage the population numbers becomes a social issue for the broader and global community.

Public perception and lobbying influences political positions, policies, decisions and legislation. Lobby movements can operate on a local, state, national or international scale. Lobbying can be led by scientific, community or business organisations that seek to influence a position or response from government. You may identify that lobbying to promote understanding of an issue, such as the management of kangaroo populations, and to influence an outcome will be important in order to make progress. Government seeks input on policy or planning through public consultation, inquiries and surveys. Your plans will help inform your participation in these processes.

The economic climate will also affect your situation and decision-making. You may be concerned with employment, competition, capital and resources, as well as markets, interest rates, land values, taxes and the impacts of government policy. Businesses that are resilient to economic variations have clear goals and understand the influence that factors have on their operations. Others that respond to external changes, rather than anticipate them, find it hard to be proactive and are always in a state of uncertainty.

It is important to determine what the influencing factors are, which of them are outside your control, and which you can control. This is important later when considering what actions to implement. Our own attitude and practices are factors under our control. But we can try to influence the understanding and attitude of others through awareness, experience and education – whether relating to science, politics or community.

Not taking these factors into account may hinder you from influencing the issues that are impacting you and your ability to take positive action. Fully understanding these factors allows you to understand what influence, positive or negative, may be underlying the issues affecting you.

ACTION: WORK WITH YOUR TEAM

It is often a useful exercise to consider the scientific, social and political factors that are influencing your current situation.

- What scientific information is currently available that helps explain the situation?
- Are there gaps in or limitations to the scientific information?
- Are there social perceptions or movements that affect your situation?
- What are the influential political or legislative factors?
- What are the economic considerations affecting you?

Philosophies

Philosophies are among the internal factors influencing individual and shared decisions. Understanding and adoption of particular schools of thought may be influenced by the greater scientific, political or social understandings. This is how values are expressed and implemented.

It is often a useful exercise to unpack your thought process.

How do your thoughts translate to practices?

This is not necessarily academic or deeply theoretical, just simply a question of what your viewpoints are. Consider organics, for example. What is the driving force for a farmer to adopt organic production? It might be based on deep beliefs when it comes to the use of chemicals or it might be in pursuit of a market opportunity. I work with an intensive animal enterprise that practices organic farming to satisfy their own business philosophy for animal production and meet customer demand from those who share the same values. Groups of farmers are now getting together who share philosophies, such as being organic, to collectively market their products to likeminded customers.

This is an opportunity to determine where there is common ground in schools of thought. Identifying differences in philosophy is an opportunity to explore the team's current understandings and approaches.

What are the experiences and outcomes that have been achieved with the different approaches?

What can we learn? How can we share?

Can we come to an agreement regarding a certain approach?

Often, farmers in a local area will have attended the same courses, field days or extension activities. They might be exposed to industry or government-led initiatives or programs, or private service providers. Farmers will be drawn to programs that relate to their values, inform their position and support their philosophy.

A Landcare Group I work with started planting trees with the hope of distributing 2,000 trees to forty landholders over two years. Their aim was to raise awareness of koala presence in the local area and support landholders to increase the connectivity of koala habitat. Five years later, the group has planted over 9,000 trees, involving over 100 landholders, and has locked in a further four years and 7,000 trees. There was a shared value across the landholders in the district that was not commonly discussed. The project allowed people to chat about the importance of koalas and put trees back in the landscape. This was meaningful not just for each person or property, but the whole district.

The process of strategic and management planning should inform your current understanding and help you explore appropriate approaches to management practices. Philosophies may be challenged or supported, depending on your team's situation.

FUTURE FARM BLUEPRINT

ACTION: WORK WITH YOUR TEAM

It is often a useful exercise to consider the thoughts, understanding and practices that are influencing current management.

- Are there particular schools of thought or programs that describe or influence your current management approach?

ACTION: WRITE YOUR STRATEGIC PLAN

Heading: Our values

Add to the values section by grouping economic, environmental and social values under headings as appropriate.

Further to the values section, add a note on 'guiding principles' if there are identifiable aspects that drive your decision-making.

CHAPTER 4

Setting Twenty-Year Goals

This chapter will look at identifying what assets are important to your business, their current condition and what future state you would like them to be in. It might be difficult to set specific goals for a date, say, twenty years from now, but describing the ideal situation provides clear direction and something to aim towards. Visualising the end state helps identify the smaller, shorter-term actions that will make progress towards the goal.

The Farm Logic Map at the strategic level will be constructed. The logic map visually presents all the assets and their desired future state, links to the vision, and provides a framework to map the best approach to achieving it. Essentially, this is your blueprint.

What are the assets?

There are generally five broad areas that assets can be grouped under in the context of sustainable farming. These are:

1. Natural resources
2. Production
3. Built
4. Business
5. People

NATURAL RESOURCES are the foundational assets of your farm. They have both environmental and production functions and values. Broadly speaking, they are landforms, soils, water, plants, animals, sun, microbes, air, etc. Together they contribute to ecosystems, landscapes, biodiverse communities, climate and carbon cycling, etc. Every part of the world has its own unique combination of parts interacting as a whole.

What is the unique environment of your farm? Describe the key natural resource assets.

What assets are important for you to protect, manage or repair?

PRODUCTION ASSETS are how you use natural resources to generate income for your farming business. These might be grazing, cropping, horticulture, intensive animal production, aquaculture, timber, bee keeping, etc. They might even include quarry materials, natural gas, solar energy, and feral or native animal harvesting.

Thinking forward twenty years, the ability of the natural assets to sustain production activities is valued more, compared to the actual commodity or product itself.

What production systems optimise your farm assets? What are the key production assets?

BUILT ASSETS are simply the infrastructure that supports the production system, business or people. Infrastructure interacts directly with the natural environment, is foundational to the business operations and future capabilities, and supports lifestyle. Built assets might include buildings, roads, yards and processing plants, as well as machinery and the application of technology.

What are the built assets that are essential to your farm? Why are they important?

The BUSINESS ASSETS relate to the business structure, operations, assets, intellectual property, finances, profitability, markets, industry security, employment and access to services. The business is the entity through which you make decisions about how to manage your production system and natural assets for financial outcomes.

What are the key assets of your business? Describe the ideal future position of the business.

PEOPLE ASSETS relate to how people connected to the farm are valued. They address their relationships, experiences, knowledge, skills and talents, ambitions, lifestyles and wellbeing. They acknowledge the importance of past, present and future culture and heritage. They also recognise the broader connection that people and communities have to the presence and management of the farm assets, even if they are not directly associated with it.

Who are the key people connected to your farm? How are they valued and how do they value the farm?

How would you describe the future connection people have with the farm?

Identifying the main assets of the farm allows a very complex and integrated system to be broken down into its functioning parts. Starting your plan by looking at assets, rather than issues, allows for a more positive footing from which to address the issues later on. While developing the plan, the team will gain more clarity around and understanding of the complexity of the system, increasing appreciation of past efforts.

ACTION: WORK WITH YOUR TEAM

With the team, identify the key assets, broadly considering the five asset areas:

1. Natural resources
2. Production
3. Built
4. Business
5. People

ACTION: FARM LOGIC MAP

On the Farm Logic Map:

1. Write the five asset headings on five sheets of A5 paper and spread them out horizontally across the top of the logic map.

2. For each of the asset areas, write the broad assets, with one on each piece of paper. Break down into sub-assets linking to the core asset if appropriate. For example, the core asset of water can be split into surface and ground water.

3. For proposed new operations or developments, map these on different colour paper (shown outlined below).

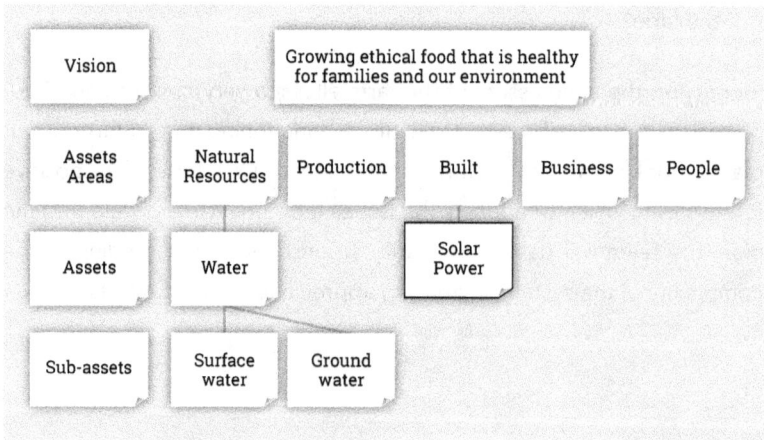

Farm Logic Map 3: Assets (Level 2) Example

The ideal state

The ideal state refers to what you want an asset to look like in twenty years' time. Setting specific and measurable goals far into the future can seem like an abstract exercise. But describing what it looks like, how it will be used or the condition it will be in helps you to visualise and connect with the long-term outcome.

For each of the assets identified in the previous section, what is their optimal condition?

What does being 'sustainable' look like for each of these assets?

Think about the asset and visualise it as if you were already in the future. If you were to describe each asset:

How would it be functioning?

What is its condition, state or behaviour?

These statements should be positive and written in the present tense. Descriptive statements are often more meaningful than any numeric measures at this level. For example: The creek is swimmable; fish are plentiful; runoff is clear.

'Issues' have still not been raised or addressed at this point. The next planning stages will identify the impacts on the assets and the approach to take. But at this level, you should understand and identify what is important and why you want to protect, maintain, restore or improve the condition of your assets. This method helps to put the impacts into perspective and make the purpose of your business and its future goals positive.

If you are focused on issues and addressing the impact of threatening processes, it can be draining and negative. There are many frustrations and challenges associated with farming, as it can be influenced by things outside your control. By turning the long-term goals into positive outcomes, you can feel connected to the valuable contribution you will have made. It puts you in control of your destination. This is, of course, achieved by managing the impacts, but a spin at the strategic level can be motivating for the team. People want to make a positive contribution and feel rewarded for their effort.

The ideal state forms the basis for setting long-term goals for the business. How to write the goals will be addressed shortly. At this level, it is worth trying to be specific about each of the assets, detailing why they are important and what their future state looks like. This will form a deeper connection and motivate the team to properly plan how to go about achieving it. Broad statements like 'sustainable production', 'functioning environment', 'profitable business' or 'happy people' need to be broken down further.

ACTION: WORK WITH YOUR TEAM

Discuss the desired state or condition for each of the assets and agree on a statement that describes it. The ideal states will be written up as goals in the next section.

Writing sustainability goals

Your farm strategic plan should be starting to take form. The purpose of the business is clear, you have a shared vision and the team has gained clarity about what is important to them and why. The underlying values have been identified and recognised as informing how you will operate and do business to achieve your goals. You have described the assets that are the foundation of the business and what a sustainable future might look like. Now you will make overarching and guiding commitments to this vision by setting goals for the future.

Sustainability is not just a motherhood statement, nor an end state. It is a continual process of improving and refining a production system within the capacity of the natural resources to sustain it. Production is limited by the condition of natural resources. Some production elements will be finite, such as extracting quarry materials and natural gas, as the time for regeneration is well beyond our lifetime. However, the regeneration cycle for soils, pasture, trees and surface water can be much shorter.

Long-term performance is also governed by the management of the fiscal business, the knowledge and capacity of the people, and the supporting infrastructure.

In terms of sustaining a profitable production system, what is the ideal condition or function of your natural resources within their regenerative capacity? What is the ideal state of the business, infrastructure and people?

To set goals in the strategic plan, you simply need to express the future description for each asset in a clearly defined statement. Goals should generally be SMART, i.e. Specific, Measurable, Achievable, Realistic and Time-bound.

Being SPECIFIC means describing the scope and scale of the asset and detailing what the condition, state, function or behaviour is. Think of it like a drone looking down on the property in twenty years' time: What would it see? Zoom in and zoom out. For example, at the property scale, you might identify that 'soils are healthy and productive'. Now zoom in to describe what this specifically means, e.g. 'soil types are physically, nutritionally and biologically balanced within their characteristics'. You can go on to describe what the optimal condition is based on soil type and use (e.g. pastures, cropping).

Being MEASURABLE means describing the state or condition in a way that enables a change from present to future to be understood or visualised. In the example, what are the measures for soil that indicate the physical state, nutrition/chemical state, and biological features? You might measure these with pH, organic matter, trace elements and water infiltration capacity. There are many measurable characteristics of soil. So, it is helpful to consider indicator measures. For example, organic matter is an indicator of biological activity and carbon content and assumes improved soil structure and water infiltration capacity.

Setting ACHIEVABLE goals means exactly that. You are only considering goals twenty years out, which are TIME-BOUND. Think back twenty years to what has happened within your production system in that time. Sustainability is a continual process. Put limitations on your goals based on what is actually achievable within the capacity of the natural resources, business and people to change their condition over a twenty-year period. You will revise and set new goals for the future as you move towards your vision.

Being REALISTIC takes achievability one step further and considers the likelihood of change actually occurring. Desiring an ideal state for any of the assets does not necessarily mean it is likely to be achieved.

I recommend setting broad, whole-of-farm goals per asset first, and then breaking them down based on area or function. Use the Farm Logic Map to do this, showing the relationship and the logic behind the goal. The goal of 'Healthy and productive soils' will be made up of many more detailed goals which are linked to the success of other goals to do with water and pasture.

ACTION: WORK WITH YOUR TEAM

Go through the following process to set an overarching goal for each of the assets. Replace the asset name and description with the final goal on the logic map. Then produce a sub-set of goals for each asset that reflects the level of detail that is useful for you.

- What is the desired state of the asset in twenty years' time?
- How will the state be measured?
- Is it achievable?
- Is it realistic?

ACTION: FARM LOGIC MAP

Use the Farm Logic Map to identify the core assets, goals and connections so you can capture the detail in your strategic plan.

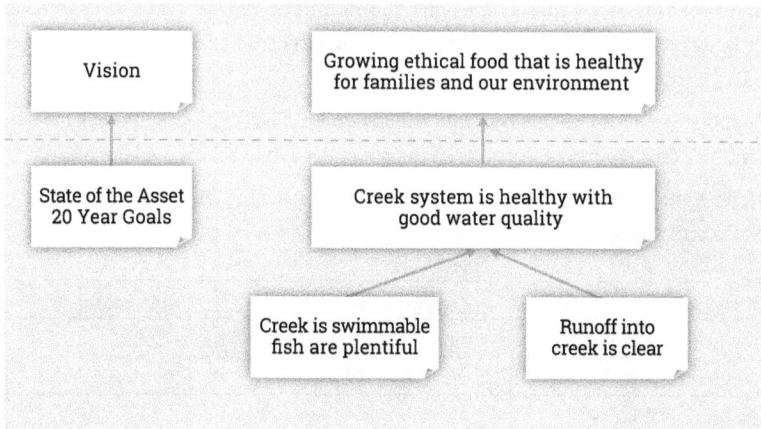

Farm Logic Map 4: Asset Goals (Level 2) Example

ACTION: WRITE YOUR STRATEGIC PLAN

Heading: Key farm assets

Write a list of your assets in a table as follows, differentiating between core assets and sub-assets.

Asset area	Core assets	Sub-assets
Natural resources		
Production		
Built		
Business		
People		

Heading: Asset twenty-year goals

At the strategic planning level, the knowledge and information to set specific and measurable targets have not been covered yet. Write descriptive statements to start with, then come back and refine the goals further as described in later planning steps. This stage is about direction and identifying all the parts of the business.

Responses should be positive, and the statements written in the present tense. Link the description of the state of the asset to each asset on the logic map.

Write your goals in a table as follows, differentiating between overarching goals and sub goals.

Asset area	Overarching goal	Sub-goals
Natural resources		
Production		
Built		
Business		
People		

Case study: Paige Pastoral

Paige Pastoral – Strategic Plan

1. ABOUT THE PLAN

Purpose of the Plan: Paige Pastoral has prepared this strategic plan to set out our future goals and give direction to our management decisions. This plan describes our pursuit of a vibrant and sustainable agricultural business and the contribution of our people to this vision.

Who it is for: This plan has been prepared and adopted by Mark and Jane Paige, and Nigel and Mary Paige, as Directors of Paige Pastoral, and Bill Long, as farm manager. Each member of our team is an equal player and decisions and actions are conducted in collaboration.

This plan will be used by the team as an internal document and may guide communication and engagement with others.

Stakeholders: Paige Pastoral values the contribution and support of other organisations and businesses to realise the intentions of this plan. In the implementation of this plan, we will collaborate with service provides such as our agents and advisors, our local Landcare group, government agencies and our neighbours.

About Us: Paige Pastoral specialises in organic grass-fed beef production. All land is under a rotational grazing system focused on groundcover, biodiversity, soil health and animal performance.

The business has grown from the original family property when a second property was purchased in 2002 and a third property in 2009. The properties were acquired in poor health caused by overgrazing and prolonged drought. The current system of pasture management has seen a marked improvement in production capacity and health of the land.

The Paige Pastoral team includes owners Mark and Jane Paige, Nigel and Mary Paige and property manager Bill Long. There is a succession plan in place that will see Mark and Jane retire within ten years.

2. OUR WHY

Paige Pastoral is a family-oriented business that provides for our families and staff and the broader community. We strive to operate our production systems in a way that is sustainable and culminates in nourishing and high-quality food. Nurturing and regenerating the environment is important to us as stewards of the land. We deeply respect our animals and their welfare.

Our Vision: Paige Pastoral is a profitable family business producing delicious premium organic grass-fed beef that is healthy for local families and the environment.

3. OUR VALUES

People
- Work as a cohesive team.
- Utilise and build our skills, talents and areas of interest.
- Conduct business and life in a way that supports health, happiness and a comfortable lifestyle.
- Respect one another and others.
- Actively support our community.

Environment

- Be responsible environmental custodians.
- Manage land within its capability.
- Hold high standards for animal welfare.

Economic

- Maintain financial health that supports all endeavours.
- Continually improve management.
- Uphold good governance and succession.
- Drive innovation and technological advancements.

Guiding principles

- We practise sustainable, integrated and regenerative approaches to land management.
- We have adopted 100% organic and grass-fed beef production.
- We encourage self-reliance and sustainability on farm.

4. ASSETS

Asset Area	Core assets	Sub-assets
Natural Resources	Climate	Rainfall, temperature, sunlight
	Carbon	
	Biodiversity	Flora, fauna
	Vegetation	Woodlands, pastures
	Water	Creeks, groundwater
	Land systems	Land resource areas, soil types
Production	Grazing system	Pastures, livestock
Built	Water system	Dams, bores, pipes, troughs, telemetry
	Fencing	Boundary pest fencing, internal fencing
	Buildings	Shed, workshop, houses
	Machinery	Tractor, vehicles
	Technology	Monitoring equipment

Asset Area	Core assets	Sub-assets
Business	Intellectual property	Genetics, grazing system
	Markets	Local organic market
	Operating systems	Finances, governance, procedures, plans
	Industry	Best management practice, legislation
	Service providers	Agent, nutritionist, accountant etc.
People	Business	Family, manager, contractors, casual
	Attributes	Skills, knowledge, experience, networks
	Wellbeing	Lifestyle, health, culture, heritage
	Community	Local, global, industry

5. TWENTY-YEAR GOALS

Asset Area	Core asset	Goals
Natural Resources: Natural resources are valued as part of a healthy, adaptive, biodiverse and functioning ecosystem	Climate	Renewable energy production sustains our needs Production is enhanced within the variability of local climate conditions
	Carbon	Carbon is sequestered and valued
	Biodiversity	Habitats support abundant local flora and fauna within a balanced system
	Vegetation	Vegetation supports core habitats and linkages in the landscape Timber harvesting selectively enhances habitats and grazing systems
	Water	The creek system is healthy, swimmable and abundant with fish Water resources are used efficiently and of good quality Water running off the farm is clear
	Land Systems	Land systems are used within their capability Soils are protected and healthy and have high organic matter

Asset Area	Core asset	Goals
Production: Land use is optimised within its capabilities for production of organic, grass-fed beef	Grazing	Produce quality organic beef Pastures are diverse and healthy, with 100% cover Animals are cared for and healthy
Built: Technology, machinery and infrastructure optimised business operations	Technology	Technology is embraced to optimise operations
	Machinery	Machinery is purposeful and optimised
	Infrastructure	Built infrastructure is purposeful and maintained Stock water systems are efficient
Business: The business is profitable, robust, evolving and conducted with integrity	IP	Intellectual property is documented and valued
	Markets	Markets align with business goals Sustained price for local, premium, organic, grass-fed beef
	Operating systems	Profit sustains the business and people Succession plans in place
	Industry	Industry expectations are exceeded
	Service providers	External advice and services add value to business goals
People: People are capable and enjoy a healthy lifestyle with connection to the community	Family	People are valued, skilled and capable
	Staff	We have a culture of learning and continual improvement Families are supported, healthy and we are happy
	Community	Actively support and engage with the local and broader community

64

6. FARM LOGIC MAPS

Asset Goals

Vision

Paige Pastoral is a profitable family business producing delicious premium organic grass-fed beef that is healthy for local families and the environment.

State of the Asset 20 Year GOALS

Natural Resources are valued as part of a healthy, adaptive, biodiverse and functioning ecosystem	Land use is optimised within its capabilities for the production of organic, grass-fed beef	Technology, machinery and infrastructure optimise business operations	The business is profitable, robust, evolving and conducted with integrity	People are capable and enjoy a healthy lifestyle with connection to the community

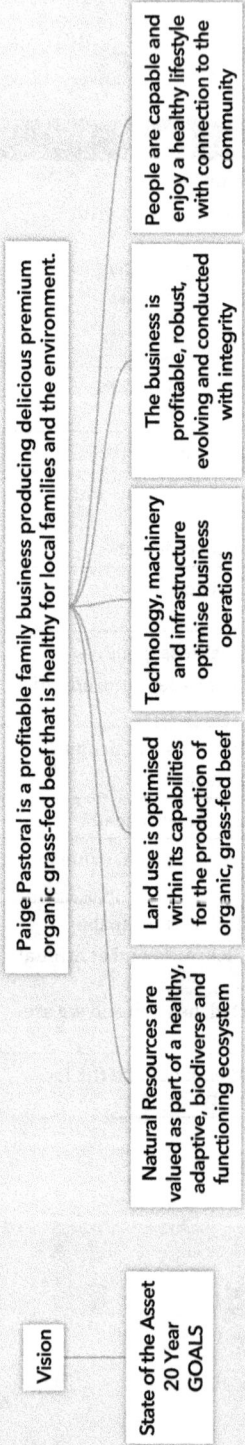

Asset Goals (Level 2) - Overarching

Vision

Paige Pastoral is a profitable family business producing delicious premium organic grass-fed beef that is healthy for local families and the environment.

State of the Asset 20 Year GOALS

Natural Resources are valued as part of a healthy, adaptive, biodiverse and functioning ecosystem

State of the sub-asset 20 Year GOALS

Renewable energy production sustains our needs

Production is enhanced within the variability of local climate conditions

Carbon is sequestered and valued

Vegetation supports core habitats and linkages in the landscape

Water quality is protected
- Water running off farm is clear
- Creeks are healthy, swimmable and abundant with fish

Land systems are used within their capability
- Soils are protected and healthy with high organic matter and biological activity

Asset Goals (Level 2) - Natural Resources

Vision

Paige Pastoral is a profitable family business producing delicious premium organic grass-fed beef that is healthy for local families and the environment.

State of the Asset 20 Year GOALS

Land use is optimised within its capabilities for the production of organic, grass-fed beef

State of the sub-asset 20 Year GOALS

Quality beef is produced and organic certified

Animals are cared for and healthy

Pastures are diverse and healthy, with 100% cover

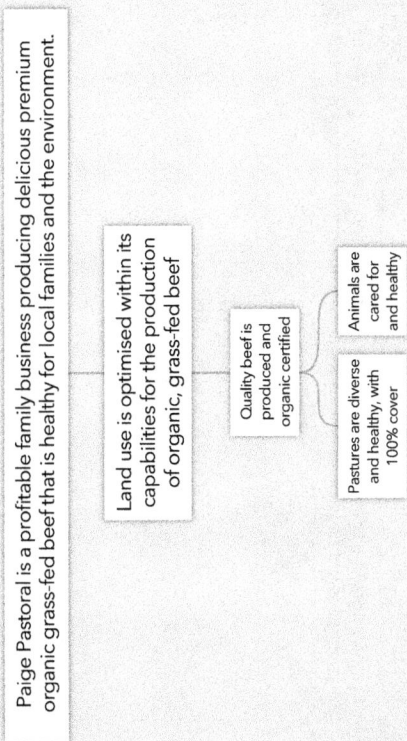

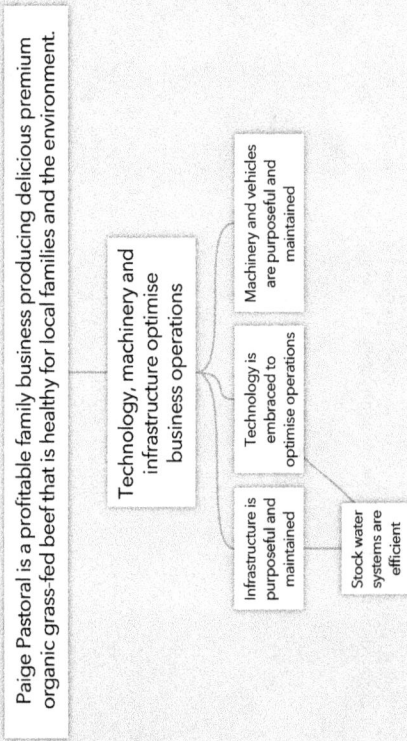

Asset Goals (Level 2) - Production

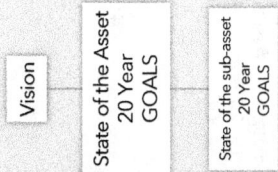

Vision

Paige Pastoral is a profitable family business producing delicious premium organic grass-fed beef that is healthy for local families and the environment.

State of the Asset 20 Year GOALS

Technology, machinery and infrastructure optimise business operations

State of the sub-asset 20 Year GOALS

Machinery and vehicles are purposeful and maintained

Technology is embraced to optimise operations

Infrastructure is purposeful and maintained

Stock water systems are efficient

Asset Goals (Level 2) - Built

Vision

Paige Pastoral is a profitable family business producing delicious premium organic grass-fed beef that is healthy for local families and the environment.

State of the Asset 20 Year GOALS

The business is profitable, robust, evolving and conducted with integrity

State of the sub-asset 20 Year GOALS

- IP is documented and valued
- Markets align with business goals
  - Sustained price achieved for local, premium organic beef
- The business operates with high degree of efficency
- Profit sustains the business and people
  - Succession plans in place
- Industry expectations are exceeded
- External advice and services add value to the business goals

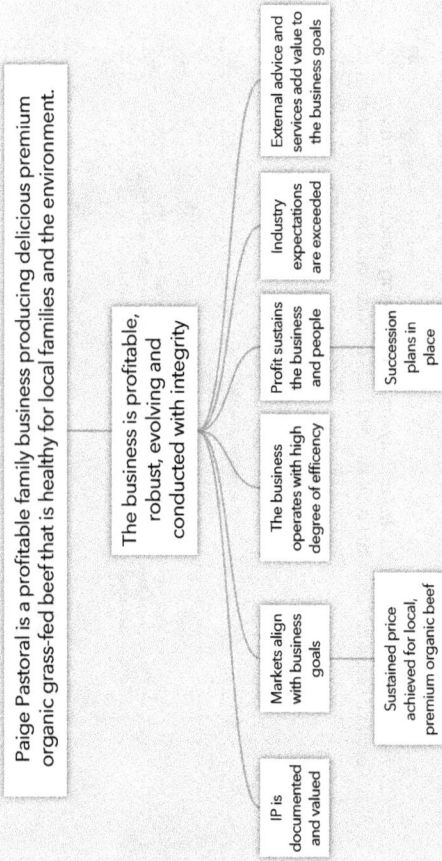

Asset Goals (Level 2) - Business

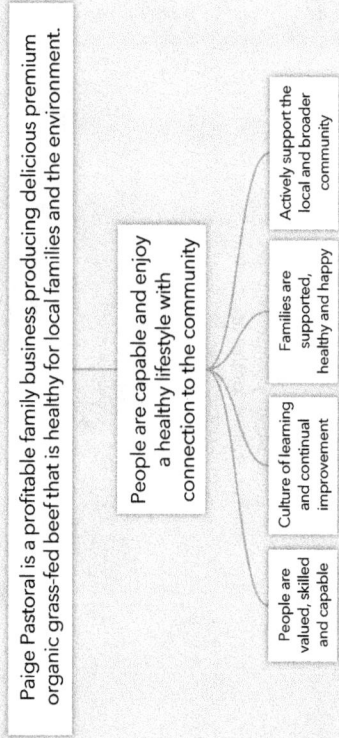

Vision

Paige Pastoral is a profitable family business producing delicious premium organic grass-fed beef that is healthy for local families and the environment.

State of the Asset 20 Year GOALS

People are capable and enjoy a healthy lifestyle with connection to the community

State of the sub-asset 20 Year GOALS

- People are valued, skilled and capable
- Culture of learning and continual improvement
- Families are supported, healthy and happy
- Actively support the local and broader community

Asset Goals (Level 2) - People

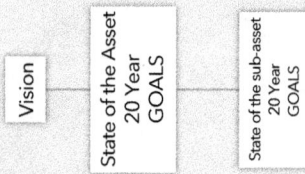

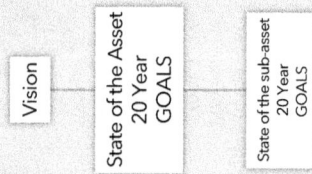

You now have a Future Farm Strategic Blueprint that outlines your desired destination in twenty years' time. It provides clarity across the business team about why sustainability is important, the overall vision for the farm and the underpinning values that will drive decisions along the way.

Part two will start to look at how you are going to achieve your goals and set the Management Blueprint for your farm.

PART 2

KNOWLEDGE

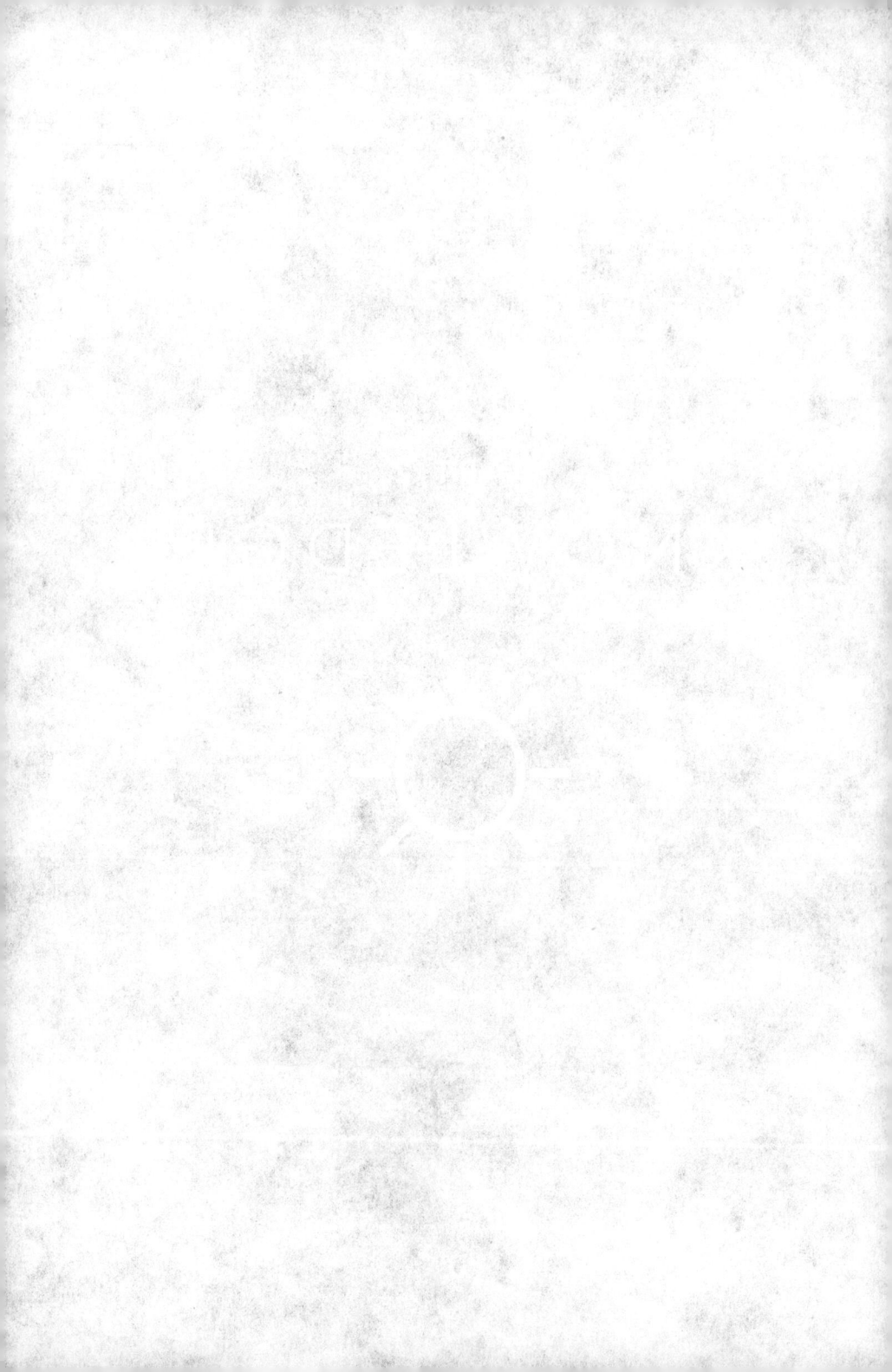

CHAPTER 5

Future Farm Management Blueprint

Like any journey, the route needs to be mapped out to make sure you are heading in the right direction and that potential obstacles along the way have been identified and the risks mitigated. The longer the journey, the greater the possibility there will be unexpected setbacks. Setting waypoints, such as five-year milestones, helps you measure progress and assess if your actions are making headway towards your bigger-picture intentions. A written management plan will help you to be clear about the agreed pathway and avoid unhelpful detours along the way.

A MANAGEMENT PLAN documents what is understood about the current situation and seeks to inform farm management decisions. This enables you to take the best approach towards realising the long-term goals. It demonstrates the underlying logic that supports the leap from small actionable steps to significant improvements or changes in the state of the assets.

A management plan focuses on the knowledge that informs how you will achieve your sustainability goals. The plan itself doesn't necessarily document the full process you will undertake, but it should demonstrate how decisions are made about the best approach to take and why.

The components of a management plan include a recap of the long-term goals against each of the core assets, to demonstrate the link to shorter-term milestones. These milestones are referred to as management goals and describe the desired state of the asset in five years' time. A range of management strategies are then developed based on relevant information. Performance indicators are identified to help measure success.

Setting long-term goals and then proceeding to undertake short-term activities is a mistake often made with planning and presents risks to the business. The leap from business objectives and goals to implementing on-ground activities is a large one and leaves room for diversions and distractions. A management plan will specifically guide what short-term actions to take in order to achieve the long-term goals. It takes the guesswork out of what to invest in and why.

The following chapters focus on the knowledge that helps you to critically assess and understand your current farm situation and identify the best strategies for achieving five-year milestones. A management planning process is a concentrated effort into strategic decision-making. This enables the implementation of appropriate and effective annual action plans.

Why do you need a management plan?

A management plan sets five-year SMART goals (Specific, Measurable, Achievable, Realistic and Time-bound goals) for each of your identified assets. It breaks the long-term goals into specific and achievable milestones. Current information, influencing factors and experience inform

the development of strategies for a high-confidence approach to progress towards the goals. These strategies guide short-term action plans.

A management plan is a guiding document that makes more-strategic
decisions and takes a longer-term view of the delivery of actions. It considers
a wide range of factors, addressing what can be done, what makes a chosen
approach a good approach and the level of confidence you can have that
it will succeed.

The process of preparing the components of a management plan is
important for the team. The team will share and review what is currently
understood and identify any gaps in knowledge that may be pertinent to
changing the status quo. This may trigger further investigation into what
others are doing in the industry or flag areas for new research and innovation. If there are varying attitudes towards the current situation, it might
be useful to explore how attitudes differ and what is influencing this.

This initial research will also flag important industry standards, legislation
or community expectations and other information that might influence
what and how actions can be undertaken. Identifying these considerations upfront will guide decisions and help avoid any problems that
could cause concern for your business.

Jumping straight to an action plan from the strategic plan will likely mean
you miss some key considerations. There is a tendency when making
action plans to do what is familiar or what has been done previously. Such
plans are also often focused on issue-management tasks, as opposed
to asset protection. The management planning process enables you to
justify your decisions and communicate them to others with confidence.

It is likely you are familiar with the elements of a management plan, which
may traditionally be reported in a strategic plan or action plan. However,

I encourage you to separate these elements out and specifically set management goals and strategies for the assets. It helps if the plan is documented separately as it falls into a different period for review, monitoring and evaluation.

ACTION: WORK WITH YOUR TEAM

Discuss with the team why a management plan is important and the benefits of having an agreed plan. This discussion will inform the purpose of the plan.

- What are the benefits of setting five-year management goals for the assets?
- What are the benefits of investigating the best approach to achieve the goals?

What is the purpose of your management plan?

The purpose of a management plan is to document the agreed short-term goals and the management strategies required to achieve them. It is designed to support decisions with knowledge of the best approach you can take in order to achieve your long-term goals.

A management plan breaks each of the long-term goals for the assets into shorter, more manageable and achievable goals. It helps to scope the full extent of the problem in relation to a goal and makes room for new thought and information. A risk assessment is conducted to test the level of confidence in the strategies and improve the likelihood that the delivery mechanisms will be successful. The management goals offer a reference point with which to validate the approaches taken and the progress of actions.

The team can consistently and confidently communicate their management strategies to external stakeholders, keeping them informed. Having a well-researched and planned approach will strengthen the business position, attracting valuable partners, investors and market opportunities. A thorough understanding of the influencing factors will allow you to take control of your ability to influence change and perceptions.

The plan can be used to demonstrate the linkages across the farm operations to other programs or plans. Industry programs, local funded projects, council programs, etc. will be specific to their own needs. Using your Farm Logic Map, you can see where your farm planning aligns with other plans and programs. This can otherwise be difficult to do, leading to confusion and often duplication of effort, particularly in relation to reporting. The management plan acknowledges the complexity of the systems in which you work and identifies where one strategy might contribute to several goals.

ACTION: WORK WITH YOUR TEAM

Scope the purpose of the management plan with the team.

- How will a management plan be used internally?
- How will a management plan be used externally?

Who will be involved?

The management plan is a useful internal document that serves to inform the decisions of the business partners, management team or staff. Management planning enables annual action planning and budgeting to be much more efficient, effective and focused.

As with the Strategic Plan, you need to consider who is involved in the development and implementation of the plan. The nature of the planning often requires input from other relevant sources to help understand the full extent of the situation and influencing factors.

The team can use the plan to inform their own actions and understand their contribution to the outcomes. It is a great tool with which to pass responsibility to members of the team. When people understand and have ownership over what the business is working towards, they are in a better position to look forward and prioritise tasks, rather than wait to be told what to do next. Every small task has a place and the plan can show how it contributes to something important.

It is worth taking some time to consider the specific people that will be involved with management planning.

ACTION: WORK WITH YOUR TEAM

Identify the target audiences and roles in relation to the management plan.

- Who has ownership of the plan?
- Who has an interest in the plan?
- What level of engagement is appropriate for each person?
- Who is responsible for overseeing delivery of the plan?

Clearly communicate with each audience their intended role and participation in the development of the management plan.

ACTION: WRITE YOUR MANAGEMENT PLAN

Heading: Purpose of the Plan
Describe in the opening section of the farm management plan what the plan will document and how the plan will be used.

Heading: Who it is for
In the introduction, provide a brief description of the key people and their connection to the plan.

CHAPTER 6

What is Currently Known?

The process of developing a management plan explores what is currently understood and seeks to build knowledge in order to implement appropriate actions in the future. It explores what is currently known about the condition of the assets, the influencing factors and the threatening processes. Through knowledge and understanding, the best-bet strategies can be developed to provide the greatest chance of achieving future goals.

The first step involves investigating what information is available about the condition of your assets and identifying gaps in current knowledge. It looks at how the condition is measured so that progress can be monitored over time. Considering the value of the assets and their current condition, the impacts and threatening processes are identified and assessed. Relevant information from a range of sources will help determine the appropriate action to take and the potential factors that will influence this.

This stage in the planning process is essential for ensuring that decisions about what action to take are based on relevant and robust information, with supporting evidence. It aims to address the root cause of impacts to assets and not just the symptoms. It will provide your business with a good foundation from which to meet current standards and expectations relevant to your industry and make action planning more structured and purposeful.

Asset condition assessment

In order to realise the goals set for each of the assets identified in the strategic plan, an understanding of the current condition of the assets and the degree of change needed is required. This is referred to as the asset condition assessment.

Sustainability planning is essentially change management. It is about identifying the factors that are influencing the current situation and determining different management approaches that will achieve a desired state. The first step in this process is assessing with confidence what the current condition is.

Asset condition assessments are largely factual or descriptive and based on measurable indicators. For each range of assets, there will already be commonly applied descriptions and indicators for health or condition, whether for environmental assets, production, finance and business, or people and community. The level of detail will be available at the paddock, farm, landscape or community scale. The assessment will often involve looking over the fence and more broadly at the asset, assessing its condition (describing the composition, structure and function), and seeking evidence of impacts from events, threatening processes or management.

There might already be a body of information available for your farm assets. The places to go to find out more might include government agencies, industry bodies, local groups and research organisations. You may need to refer to mapping and monitoring data, and historic farm or district records. If you are not sure where to go, identify some people who could help.

Where regionally relevant information is available, some ground-truthing, or local verification, might be required. This might involve identifying suitable indicators and undertaking sample measurements on-ground, a mapping exercise, or making correlations with other locally available data. The initial measures of condition should be as accurate as possible so that responses to changes in management can be detected and progress towards goals can be assessed.

This step might seem like a lot of work and even overwhelming if there are many assets to assess. However, guessing at or omitting current condition information while setting a future desired condition is counterproductive. Where information is missing, determining condition becomes a foundation (priority) activity to undertake in order to move forward. The more information recorded initially, the more useful future assessments will be.

You will likely be implementing actions towards goals already, but the more information there is available prior to actions being implemented, the easier it is to assess progress and determine impact. This will be addressed in more detail later, but the importance is flagged here to highlight the benefits of a thorough condition assessment.

ACTION: WORK WITH YOUR TEAM

For each asset, identify appropriate condition assessment criteria. Conduct a desktop assessment of assets and their current known condition. Assess the degree of confidence in the desktop information and determine if more thorough ground-truthing activities are required. Identify gaps in information against the criteria. Where appropriate, seek expert advice and have assessments conducted in order to increase the degree of confidence in the data and your ability to track progress.

It is often useful to conduct field tests with knowledge experts to consider asset condition. The outcomes of the assessments can be recorded in the management plan for each of the assets. It is useful to compile and record the detailed information and research that led to the outcomes in one place, such as an appendix.

Impacts on assets

Management of assets is primarily about addressing impacts from existing or potential threatening processes, events or practices. Once the condition of the asset is understood, the factors influencing that condition can be identified and options for management explored.

You often find in farm planning that the condition assessment step is skipped, and people go straight to identifying issues. However, issues need to be put in the context of your values, the impact on assets and the desired future state of the assets. Otherwise, issue management may only address the symptoms and not the cause, driven by factors over which you have no control. You may also overlook the risk of impacts in the future.

Consider soil, for example, which is a primary asset to any farm, with values associated with production and flow-on land condition. Erosion of soils is a threatening process that creates issues for production, land condition and water quality. Erosion can affect many aspects of a farming operation and degrade environmental health. When the impact of erosion on production or environmental assets can be quantified, the flow-on impact on the business or environment becomes clearer. It might be as simple as measuring the area of erosion and, therefore, potential loss for pasture or cropping, while also considering the rate of encroachment and future loss.

It is not the presence of erosion that is the issue, but the degradation of asset value, which is why one person might ignore erosion while another would wish to control it. Investment is made in prevention by under-standing soil constraints and managing them, or by undertaking repair, which may be minimal or quite extensive depending on the cause, type and severity of the erosion. A famer who assesses erosion in terms of its impact on assets in the long term, and not just the immediate cost of control, is more likely to commit to its prevention and management.

Impacts on environmental and production assets might be caused by threatening processes. These may be things like invasive animals or plants, inappropriate fire or grazing regimes, land clearing, pests or diseases, erosion, climate change, salinity, dieback, etc. Impacts might also be caused by severe weather events, such as droughts, floods, cyclones or fire, or by more subtle changes in temperature or frosts over time. Other impacts might be more closely associated with inappropriate practices, lack of suitability and capability of the land for its use, infrastructure placement, etc.

Other types of impacts might derive from policy or legislation or conflict with land use decisions. Take, for example, legislation limiting a farmer's capacity to appropriately manage regrowth and thickening vegetation in order to maintain groundcover. This greatly increases the risk of erosion and decreases the ability to control it. Conversely, clearing land for residential areas or other developments may be allowed. There are many frustrating examples where legislation or exemptions mean the intent of the legislation to protect an asset is undermined.

Business and economic asset assessments may identify internal impacts caused by practices and past decisions, or external impacts from market price, the stock market, interest rates, etc. Other prohibiting factors might include access to transport, proximity to infrastructure or availability of services. The point of this section is to help you consider what an impact is, why it is a problem and what its underlying cause might be.

- -

ACTION: WORK WITH YOUR TEAM

Identify the current impacts on or potential risks to the condition of each of the assets.

- What is the severity of the impacts or potential risk?
- What are the causes of the impacts?

- -

ACTION: FARM LOGIC MAP

Revisit the Farm Logic Map and identify the key impact for each of the assets and potential limitations to achieving the asset goals. Label the next hierarchy line down from the assets 'Impacts to assets'. Map out the impacts by linking an arrow to each of the assets they affect.

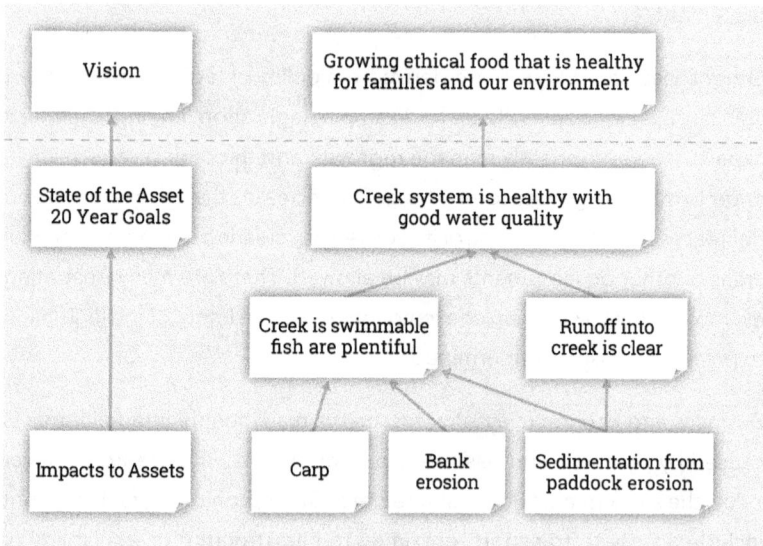

Farm Logic Map 5: Asset Impacts (Level 2) Example

- -

Relevant information

There is a range of other information that will inform the current situation and decisions about appropriate management strategies. These include broader industry, community and government expectations and requirements concerning the condition of assets and management. There might also be development of new technology or advances in genetics. Before making management decisions, it is important to understand the role and influence of external standards, legislation and developments.

Industry standards are generally established based on widespread/ common risk assessments when it comes to the protection of relevant assets. They align with government legislation and ensure that standards comply with minimum requirements. Industry programs strive for 'best practice' and are founded on a continual improvement process that ensures minimum safety, environmental, production and processing management practices are met. The programs are designed to protect the performance and social licence of industries and put in place a process to address concerns raised.

If there are industry quality assurance programs relevant to your operation, they might be a good resource from which to obtain a foundational risk assessment approach and identify mitigation strategies. The shortcoming of industry- or commodity-specific programs is the lack of integration for mixed enterprises and duplication of reporting effort. There are other, more holistic asset- and risk-assessment-based programs that might also be relevant to your business. It is worth researching the purpose of any given program, and then assessing whether it aligns with the aspirations for your farm as identified earlier in the strategic plan. This will help you find a starting point for assessing condition and impacts. Programs can be useful tools, but they may not offer a fully integrated and holistic approach, which is why this separate planning process is beneficial.

Depending on your situation, there might be external policy or social pressures based on a perception about your farm, industry or asset management. At this point, it is helpful to understand these pressures by looking into what the perception is, who holds it and why. These circumstances might be highly emotive for you; break it down so the situation is easier to assess and manage, if warranted.

What values are at stake and how are they different from yours?

The earlier example of managing plague populations of kangaroos highlights the perceptions held by different sectors of the community. Farmers are trying to reduce grazing impacts for more sustainable management of resources and are also concerned with the welfare of kangaroos in stressed conditions. While there are legal options for control such as harvesting or culling, any management attracts public criticism. There may be a lack of public understanding of the issues, but there is a shared concern for animal welfare. Fully understanding the situation and the external perceptions and impacts will help to identify to what extent they can be influenced or managed, which is addressed further on.

There is substantial public and private investment in research and development these days. This results in more advancements and new and improved ways of doing things than ever before.

Are you up to date with what is happening in your area or industry?

What networks are available to tap into this knowledge? What might be relevant to keep an eye out for in the future? Is it worth considering partnering with researchers or businesses to undertake trials?

What else is it important to know, understand or reference in order to inform appropriate management approaches? Is consultation necessary to further investigate or gain input? The point of this section is to highlight that information, resources and expectations exist beyond your business. These influence what action can be taken. Information might be relevant to the whole farm, to each asset, to the impacts or to the response.

ACTION: WORK WITH YOUR TEAM

Identify the types of information that are relevant and useful when making management decisions. Whom should you contact and where can you source information? It is useful to compile and record the detailed information and research in one place, such as an appendix.

ACTION: WRITE THE MANAGEMENT PLAN

Heading: Asset condition assessment
Record your asset condition assessment in a table as follows:

Asset	Condition assessment criteria	Current condition (year)	Degree of confidence (high, medium, low or more info needed)	References
Core asset				
Asset/sub-asset				

Heading: Impacts on assets
Following the asset condition assessment, identify the current and potential impacts on the assets. Describe why they are an impact and what the cause is. It is useful to compile and record the detailed information and research that led to identifying the impacts/causes in one place, such as an appendix.

Asset	Impact or threatening process	Severity of impact or level of risk	Source or cause of impact	References
Core asset				
Asset/sub-asset				

CHAPTER 7

What is the Desired Change?

This chapter will explore what change is achievable in five years. It will look at the current condition of the assets and determine what a realistic and desirable condition might look like in five years' time. This sets the five-year milestone that helps you make progress towards each long-term goal. It will consider the future state from an environmental, economic and social point of view.

The first step involves considering the total amount of change that is achievable in five years. It takes into account the current asset condition, impacts, rate of change processes, and what is realistic based on available information. The management targets should demonstrate in a measured way the degree of change towards long-term targets.

The next steps involve considering the type of change that needs to occur in order to meet the management target. A practice change is physical management of the asset or an impact on an asset that will result in a change in the asset condition. However, often before a practice change is adopted, an attitude change may be necessary which goes to the value of the asset. So, some of the five-year targets might involve progress towards a more desired attitude towards the asset and different appreciation of its value. The people whose attitude you need to influence might include staff, neighbours, industry professionals, researchers, business people, and the local or broader community. Acknowledging what is in your control and what is being influenced by external perception or policy is, therefore, important. This methodology gives you the power to identify how to lead change.

State of the asset in five years

Looking at an asset's current condition and considering the future desired state from the strategic plan, what is a realistic change in condition that could be achieved in five years? This question is the focus of this section.

You need to further consider the information that was gathered in the research phase. What is understood about the current condition of the asset?

What is the degree of difference between the current state and the desired twenty-year goal?

If the asset were effectively managed, what realistic degree of change could you achieve in five years?

If you have good condition assessment information, you should be able to apply accurate measures to describe the degree of change and future state of the asset. If condition has been flagged for further research, take an educated guess. This can be refined over time as more information is obtained. The five-year state of the asset should refer to the accumulated result of all management actions. If you were in a drone, looking down, five years in the future, what would look different in the image compared to five years before?

You will also need to consider the impacts and risks that exist. For each of the impacts identified in the Farm Logic Map, what level of reduction of that impact might be achievable in five years? How would this result in an improvement to the condition of the asset? What progress could be made in the best-case scenario? How could this change be measured and monitored?

For each asset, the rate of change will vary depending on the natural processes and threatening processes influencing its current state. Some change will be achieved through positive management or by reducing an impact. How the change is implemented will be addressed later.

The five-year timeframe attempts to set a milestone that is within reach and that makes progress towards the longer-term goal, but which requires more-strategic thinking than a short-term action plan. Describing the change in the asset, and not focusing on the issue, allows for a more positive and optimistic attitude towards making a change. The assets align with your values. It is important to protect and manage them for environmental, economic and social benefit. This goes to the core of why change is needed and makes it easier to commit to.

ACTION: WORK WITH YOUR TEAM

Discuss and make decisions, with expert input if required, concerning the state of each asset in five years' time. Describe a realistic and achievable change in the accumulative state of each asset. Consider the twenty-year goals, the current state of the assets, and the type and degree of impacts on the assets.

Practice change

Achieving the desired change in the state of an asset will usually require a change in the way it is managed. A practice change is about doing things differently in order to achieve a different result.

Practices manage both the asset and the impacts on the asset. Take practices when it comes to stocking, for example, such as rate, days and season timing. These will determine groundcover levels, recovery time and, ultimately, exposure to erosion.

What are your current practices?

How appropriate, effective and efficient are they?

Looking at the research, assess to what degree the current practices will achieve the desired five-year goals. Are there other appropriate practices which could be implemented? If known practices are achieving results, what is the extent to which they need to be implemented to reach the five-year milestone?

Practices are relevant for all assets – environmental, production, built, business and people. Practices encompass on-ground actions and decisions, and physical infrastructure. They are approaches or strategies that proactively protect an asset, manage it or restore it. They will often address a current impact or threatening process to reduce or minimise its effect on asset condition.

In selecting a certain practice, you need to consider how confident you are that it will result in the desired change. What evidence have you based the decision on? Is it past experience, success in other areas, or are you testing new methods? Every action has a consequence; it is the intention of planning to assess the likelihood of the desired result occurring. Being aware of the risks enables you to actively monitor and mitigate them.

It is important to understand how you are going to achieve your goals and it is important that you have confidence in the decisions you make. This step in the process enables you to review and assess what practices are appropriate for your farm.

While you may identify the required practices to achieve your goals, you may not always be directly responsible for enabling their implementation. This will be considered in the next chapter.

- -

ACTION: WORK WITH YOUR TEAM

Discuss and decide, with expert input if required, the most appropriate practices for the farm operations. Seek solutions that you believe, with a high degree of confidence, will deliver results.

- -

Attitude change

Practice change is very visible and directly seeks to manage the physical assets and their condition. However, the cause of problems or barriers to adoption of practice change may lie with attitudes.

Attitudes are a reflection of values, thoughts, experiences and knowledge. And attitudes directly affect behaviours. Take fire, for example. Attitude towards fire as a management tool varies significantly. Some land managers will not use fire at all, through fear, lack of experience or poor past experiences. Others, meanwhile, will burn regularly, some to the point of flicking a match and not caring to what extent they might impact their neighbours through lack of preparation or poor conditions.

Attitudes may not have been previously considered as influencing your land management. However, it's important to recognise that a reluctance to adopt proven practices may reflect a negative attitude towards change. This is relevant to all areas of the business. Think about your attitudes towards machinery maintenance, staff management, taxes, even taking a holiday.

For each of the asset areas, further consider who may hold different attitudes and what role these may play in the current adoption of practices. What is understood about the factors influencing the attitudes?

What is the desired attitude that would result in the adoption of desired practices?

You may be affected by the internal attitudes of family members, staff or service providers, or external attitudes from broader communities. The level of impact should be considered in these situations, and should inform the effort required to influence the attitudes in order to achieve a desired outcome. Understanding the factors contributing to the attitude will help determine a course of action. The closer you are to the people you wish to influence, the greater opportunity there is for change. Influencing broader community attitudes can still be done, but this usually involves a combined effort, hence the role of industry lobby groups.

Education and demonstration can influence attitudes that result from a lack of knowledge and understanding of practices. Involvement in trials and research can help overcome attitudes of doubt regarding practices. Resources and incentives can help influence the rate of change if attitude towards cost or urgency are barriers. A more active political lobbying campaign or community education and awareness campaign might be required where government decisions or social perception are having an impact. So, consider your role here.

Ignoring the underlying attitudes and behaviours that are influencing the condition of assets and how decisions about their management are made will affect your progress. People won't adopt changes and practices if they don't understand them, aren't confident in them and don't value them.

Progress requires a continual improvement of current practice, which is founded on changing attitudes and values. Crops are no longer tilled with horses, cotton is no longer handpicked, koalas are no longer a source of fur. Attitudes and, therefore, behaviours and practices, can be influenced, but respectfully. No one likes to be told they are wrong or bullied. Find common values and build your response around people's needs and mutual benefits.

ACTION: WORK WITH YOUR TEAM

Identify influential attitudes and behaviours by considering:

- What attitudes exist within your team that might vary and influence how they behave?

- For each of the asset areas, is the ability to successfully implement management programs affected by internal or external attitudes or behaviours?

- For the attitudes identified, to what extent can they be influenced through education and awareness?

CHAPTER 8

Setting Five-Year SMART Management Goals

The purpose of this chapter is to walk through how to record your management goals and the agreed approach to achieving them. The first section will look at how to describe the five-year asset condition milestones. The following sections will develop the practice and influence strategies that will support delivery of the milestones. Once these goals and strategies are developed, you can easily break down the priority tasks into annual action plans.

Setting management goals is similar to setting the long-term condition goals. It applies the same concept of the drone visualising what will be achieved in five years' time. It considers both an improvement in condition and reduction in impact. Most importantly, investments need to demonstrate clear progress towards goals. If your current management and priorities do not align with future desires, they need to be carefully evaluated. Remember, the point of planning is to provide a framework or blueprint with which to streamline decision-making towards meaningful outcomes.

Documenting your management strategies provides the opportunity to further evaluate current practices and their effectiveness and appropriateness within the scope of the plan. Revisit values to ensure everything you plan to do aligns and contributes to your overall vision. If management goals and strategies are not in alignment at this point, then your action plans and how you prioritise your effort and resources may get you no closer to your vision. This process identifies what to do more of, what to stop, and what to change within your business and operations. Change may be gradual, but it needs to be heading in the right direction.

With hard work done at the management planning phase, a high level of confidence is attained for the investment in and delivery of short-term action plans. With the goals in mind, every decision is purposeful and supported, with the team on board.

Establishing SMART management goals

As discussed, SMART goals are Specific, Measurable, Realistic, Achievable and Time-bound. A management goal aims for a reasonable amount of progress – progress that can be achieved in five years. It should visualise a change in the asset from the current state and demonstrate progress towards the twenty-year goal.

Management goals are milestones. They should be considered as stepping-stones specific to the particular journey from the current state of an asset to the twenty-year state. They describe what is going to be managed and what it will look like at a specific point in time.

To set a management goal, describe the type of change that will occur and over what area for each of the assets in the strategic plan. For example, for the long-term goal 'Physical, chemical and biological soil heath is optimised,' the management goal would be 'Gully erosion occurrence is reduced across fifty per cent of affected areas in five years.' Note, this is the 'what', 'where' and 'when', but not the 'how'. The drone test would easily see the area of erosion reduced across half of the presently affected areas and, based on current extent and past experience, the goal is reasonably achievable. Another management goal for the same asset might be to increase groundcover to ninety per cent across all areas in five years.

Go through the process of setting management goals for each of the assets. Apply the drone test, ensuring that measures are visible and describe what, where, when and how much. Next, we will address exactly how to achieve the goals.

- -

ACTION: WORK WITH YOUR TEAM

Set a SMART management goal for each of the assets. You can set broad goals, and then break it down for the sub-assets, ensuring to address each of the impacts to the assets.

- -

ACTION: FARM LOGIC MAP

Label a new hierarchy on the logic map: 'Five-year management goals'. Link each of the long-term goals with the management goals. Test the logic: If the management goal is achieved, will it directly result in or contribute to the twenty-year goal?

Note: you will find the wall is starting to get crowded. You can run through the Farm Logic Map broadly across the farm, for a whole of farm (zoom out) vision, then break it down (zoom in) to create a map for each asset area to capture the detail. You can see how crowded it is getting simply dealing with creek water quality. Use the same wall, just take a photo after each map is finished.

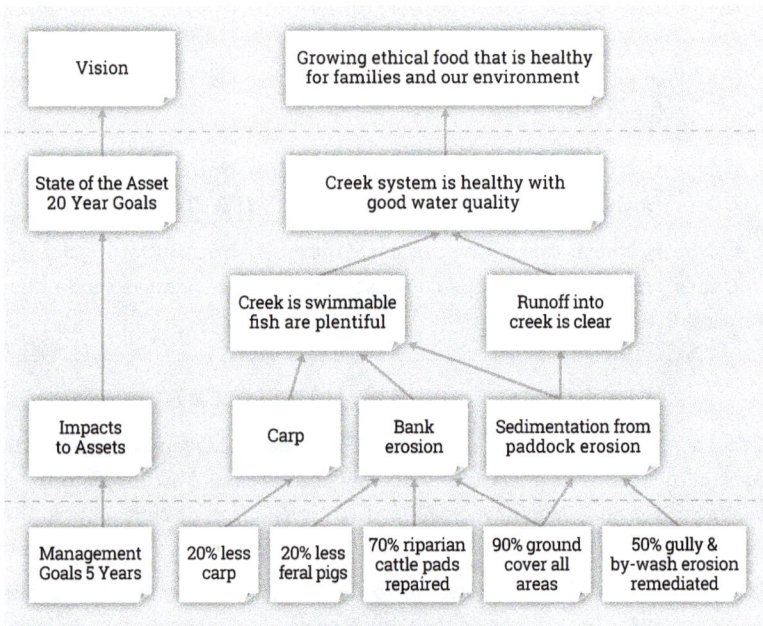

```
┌──────────┐      ┌─────────────────────────────────┐
│  Vision  │      │ Growing ethical food that is healthy │
│          │      │  for families and our environment    │
└──────────┘      └─────────────────────────────────┘

┌──────────────┐  ┌─────────────────────────────────┐
│ State of the Asset │ Creek system is healthy with   │
│ 20 Year Goals      │      good water quality         │
└──────────────┘  └─────────────────────────────────┘

                  ┌──────────────────┐   ┌──────────────┐
                  │ Creek is swimmable │   │ Runoff into   │
                  │ fish are plentiful │   │ creek is clear │
                  └──────────────────┘   └──────────────┘

┌──────────┐  ┌──────┐  ┌────────┐  ┌──────────────────┐
│ Impacts  │  │ Carp │  │ Bank    │  │ Sedimentation from │
│ to Assets│  │      │  │ erosion │  │ paddock erosion    │
└──────────┘  └──────┘  └────────┘  └──────────────────┘

┌──────────┐ ┌────────┐ ┌────────┐ ┌─────────┐ ┌──────────┐ ┌──────────┐
│Management│ │20% less│ │20% less│ │70% riparian│90% ground│50% gully &│
│Goals 5 Years│ carp  │ │feral pigs│cattle pads│cover all │by-wash erosion│
│          │ │        │ │        │ │repaired │ │areas    │ │remediated│
└──────────┘ └────────┘ └────────┘ └─────────┘ └──────────┘ └──────────┘
```

Farm Logic Map 6: Management Goals (Level 3) Example

ACTION: WRITE THE MANAGEMENT PLAN

Heading: Five-year management goals

For each of the asset areas, record your management goals in a table as follows:

Asset	Management goal	Key indicators	Level of confidence	References
Core asset				
Asset/ sub-asset				

FUTURE FARM BLUEPRINT

Establishing management strategies

Management strategies are the 'how'. They comprise the approaches that will make steps towards achieving each of the goals. There are different strategy approaches depending on the type of change you are trying to bring about, taking into consideration what is within your control and what you may be trying to influence.

Management strategies are referred to here in terms of implementing practice changes. The influence strategies in the next section address attitude changes.

Management strategies document decisions that will contribute to each of the management goals. The decision might be a one-off, such as the decision to install fencing to manage stock and pastures in order to improve groundcover, soil health and runoff water quality.

The decision might be simply to document/confirm preferred practices already implemented to maintain a beneficial situation, such as seasonally grazing creek paddocks to maintain groundcover, avoid erosion, maintain water quality and manage fire risk for that particular area.

The decision might be to effect a change in current practice, such as the decision to coordinate and control burn events and apply mosaic techniques with neighbours to reduce the risk of wildfires and their impacts on habitat, pastures, stock and infrastructure, while improving carbon sequestration.

The strategies guide short-term decisions that will be further detailed in the action plan. When considering appropriate strategies, research and risk assessment may be required to ensure there is a high degree of confidence in the approach. One strategy will often contribute to multiple goals.

Strategies should consider the research conducted, reflect the values of the team and strive to achieve the goals. You should be highly confident that results will be achieved, and the impacts should be easily measured. In order to achieve the goals, current practices must change, otherwise the desired result would already be realised. Strategies document this change, whether it's increasing the adoption of current performing strategies, stopping practices that are not serving the goals, or changing current practices.

ACTION: WORK WITH YOUR TEAM

Develop strategies that will achieve the management goals.

- What are the practices required?
- How can they be implemented?
- What is the frequency and timeframe?
- Who is involved?
- Where will practices be implemented?

In the logic map, link the practice change to the management goal that it addresses.

ACTION: FARM LOGIC MAP

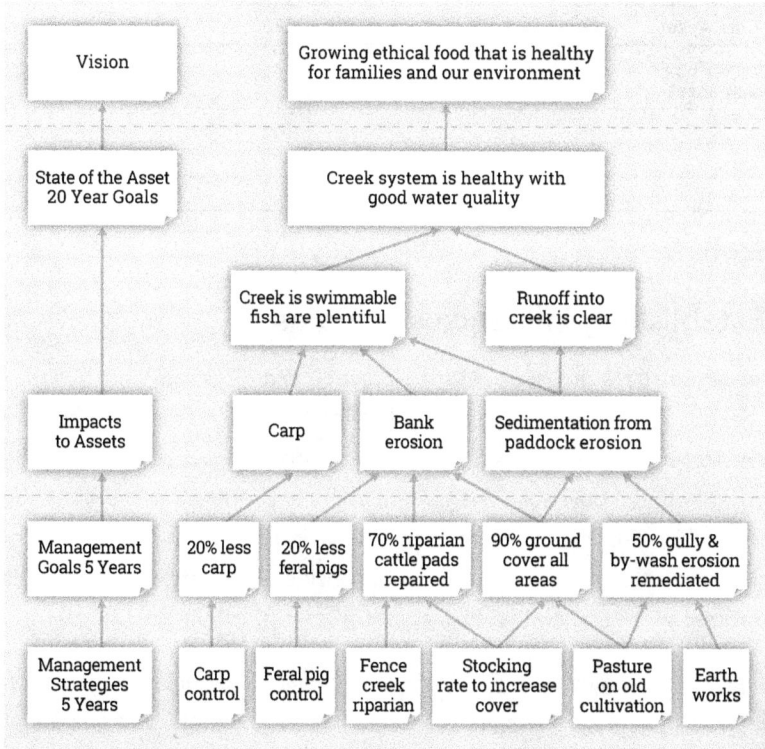

Vision	Growing ethical food that is healthy for families and our environment
State of the Asset 20 Year Goals	Creek system is healthy with good water quality

Creek is swimmable fish are plentiful	Runoff into creek is clear

Impacts to Assets	Carp	Bank erosion	Sedimentation from paddock erosion	

Management Goals 5 Years	20% less carp	20% less feral pigs	70% riparian cattle pads repaired	90% ground cover all areas	50% gully & by-wash erosion remediated

Management Strategies 5 Years	Carp control	Feral pig control	Fence creek riparian	Stocking rate to increase cover	Pasture on old cultivation	Earth works

Farm Logic Map 7: Management Strategies (Level 3) Example

- -

ACTION: WRITE THE MANAGEMENT PLAN

Heading: Five-year management goals and strategies

For each of the asset areas, record your management strategies in a table as follows:

Asset	Management goal	Management strategies	Performance indicator	References
Core Asset				
Asset/ sub-asset				

Establishing influence strategies

Influence strategies are similar to practice change strategies, but they seek to influence or change the underlying attitudes to matters affecting the achievement of goals. Throughout the book, I have drawn attention not only to the physical management of the environment and production assets but also the values, social opinions, legislation and other influential factors that need to be taken into consideration. Influence strategies address these equally important areas.

Practice strategies are quite straightforward and are generally things you can do directly to manage an asset. Influence strategies seek to affect the impact people have through their attitude, behaviour, knowledge, philosophy or experience.

Education and awareness strategies aim to influence attitudes towards or understandings of a situation. Through information exchange, they influence the basis on which current decisions are made. They might aim to influence the team's knowledge of new practices in order to achieve goals, or more broadly seek to influence public understanding and perception of practices. Education strategies should be specific about what information is extended, what influence it aims to have and who the target audience is.

Examples include hosting field days, eco-tours or educational tours. These might focus on the local community, students or interest groups. You might be trialling new technologies and want to share the results. The media might be sent articles and representatives might conduct interviews to educate the wider community. Participating in consultation and planning processes is an opportunity to influence government policy or legislation.

The achievement of management goals might be hindered by a lack of appropriate practice strategies or low confidence in the strategies. Research, investigation and planning approaches seek to inform the development of future strategies.

The formation of partnerships has the potential to influence the extent to which management goals can be achieved. Compared to operating on your own, working with partners can improve and accelerate results. Forming partnerships is an influence strategy that results in a union. It might be as simple as neighbours working together and coordinating burning or weed management practices, or it could encompass a formal connection established with industry groups for funded projects or research with universities.

All of the strategies need to consider to what extent you have direct control over the outcome of an action. There will also be external influencing factors which you will have little or no ability to influence. These might include government policy and legislation, or extreme lobby group views. Like all other strategies, influence strategies need to be assessed to determine the degree of confidence you can have in them. You need to believe the activity will lead to the desired result. This will help prioritise strategies and decide what is worth investing in.

ACTION: WORK WITH YOUR TEAM

Develop strategies that aim to influence the attitude of those impacting on the achievement of goals.

- For each of the attitudes identified, what are appropriate strategies that might influence how people think?
- How confident are you that the strategy will have an impact?
- How important is it that these attitudes are addressed?

ACTION: WRITE THE MANAGEMENT PLAN

Heading: Five-year management goals and strategies

For each of the asset areas, record your influence strategies in a table as follows:

Asset	Attitudes	Influence strategies	Performance indicator	References
Core Asset				
Asset/ sub-asset				

Your Management Plan now provides the business with clear short-term goals to work towards, enabling you to have a high level of confidence that efforts are making progress towards sustainability goals. The strategies to achieve the goals are comprehensive and address both the on-ground practices as well as other approaches that are necessary to inform and influence implementation.

In the next part of the book, the immediate action plans that need to be developed to bring these strategies to life are addressed.

PART 3

CAPABILITY

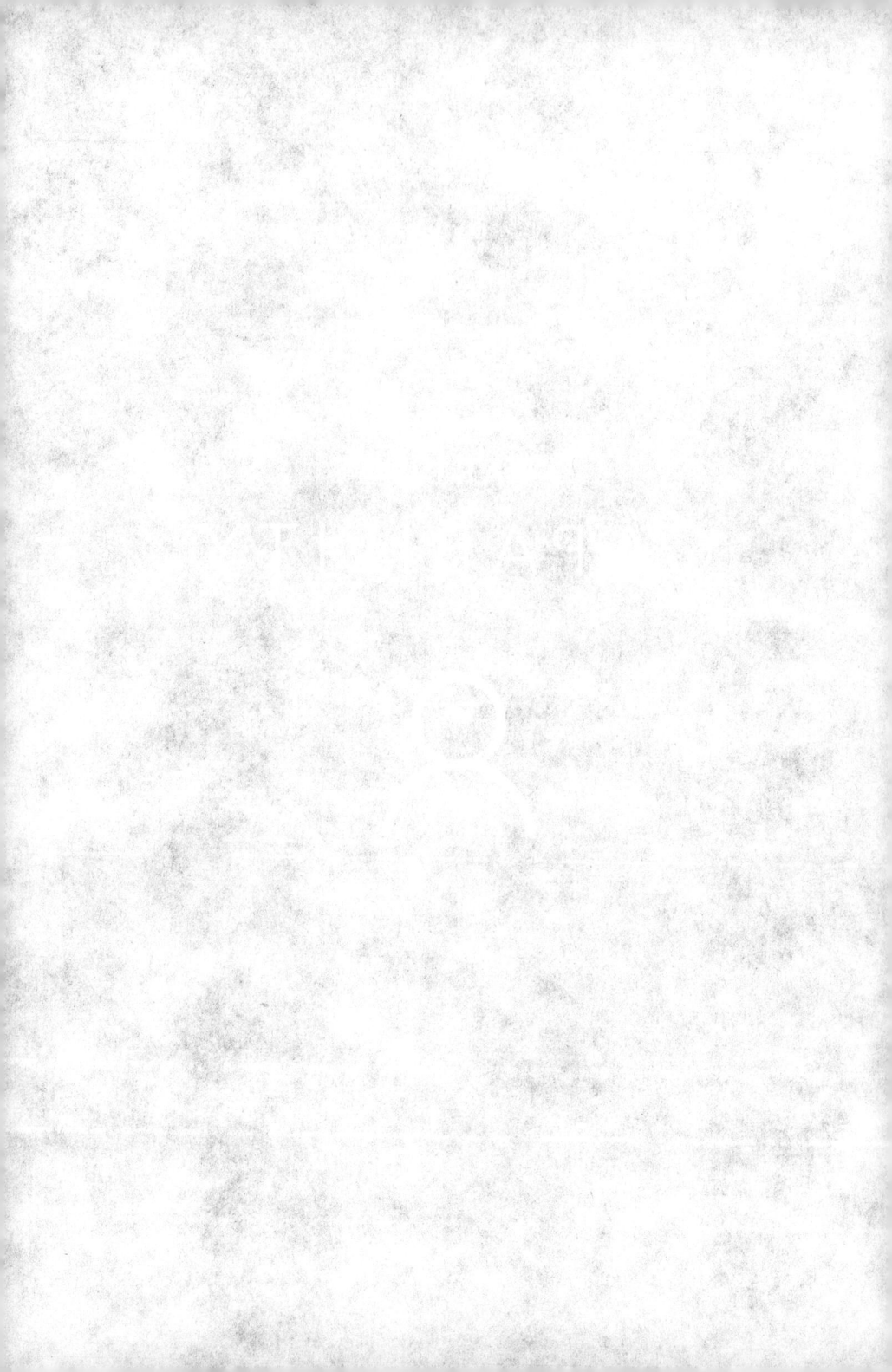

CHAPTER 9

The Future Farm Action Plan

An action plan maps out the priority steps and what is required to reach the end goal. It helps to manage the wide range of activities in the short term and focuses on the implementation of the management strategies. But simply having a plan doesn't mean you necessarily have the capability to achieve your goals. It sets you up for success but doesn't guarantee it. Delivery of the plan is essential for achieving your business purpose; being prepared and having the right expertise are important.

Part three looks at: How to prepare a delivery plan; who needs to be involved; and how to assign people to actions/tasks. It addresses how to secure resources and write grants. And it explores what it takes to keep on time and in budget, as well as covering the consequences of not managing these aspects well.

The purpose of this part of the book is to outline the different sections of an action plan, and address when to use them, what they aim to achieve and how to write them.

Why do you need an action plan?

An ACTION PLAN takes a bite-size piece of the management strategies and addresses its implementation. It applies limitations and responsibilities to ensure that you can achieve what it commits to. Most people will be familiar with an action plan, so use this section to recap and ensure your planning and implementation is effective – and actually written down.

An action plan breaks down the management strategies into logical and achievable steps. These are time-bound and dependent on the allocation of resources. The action plan allows you to take control of and responsibility for achieving your goals.

An action plan is a useful internal decision-making tool. It documents the agreed priorities and goals for the year. The team is clear about what they're aiming to achieve for the year and why, and they have a clear plan to work from. Decision-making is streamlined and more proactive, rather than reactive to opportunities and daily demands. There are expectations set around what is to be achieved and by when.

With the allocation of tasks and timeframes, team members can prioritise their own workload. Without a plan in place, the team will always be seeking direction from the lead decision-maker and waiting for permission to proceed. Staff or team members are usually highly capable, and if they have a full view of the plan ahead, they can just get on with it. Their contribution is also highly valuable when preparing the plan. Awarded more responsibility, the team is able to make decisions, respond if something unexpected comes up and get back on track again. If circumstances do change and money needs to be spent on something unexpected, resources can be reallocated and reprioritised.

With a full view of all the actions, it is easy to appreciate the consequences of doing, or not doing, particular tasks. And it is easy to appreciate how different actions affect the achievement of the business goals.

Having an action plan has external benefits as well, such as:

- Outlining legal responsibilities and the business's intention to meet requirements;
- Setting expectations with partners or service providers; and
- Positioning for investment or funding opportunities.

There is nothing more satisfying than completing an action plan, then reviewing and celebrating the achievements.

ACTION: WORK WITH YOUR TEAM

Scope why an action plan is important and the benefits of having an agreed plan.

- What are the benefits of setting one-year action plans?
- What are the benefits of investing time in detailed planning upfront?

Who is the plan for?

There are different levels of connection and responsibility associated with action plans. There is the authority role that oversees approval of decisions and expenditure of resources. There are roles responsible for planning the actions and delivering the actions. And then there are roles for those who are interested in the plan, but not involved in its implementation. Without having discussions that identify team roles, the risk is that no one takes responsibility for the preparation and delivery of the plan.

It is helpful for the people involved in delivering the plan to have a high level of input. They will understand what can reasonably be achieved within certain timeframes and what resources it will take. This also avoids conflict later when it comes to other commitments and external factors that may crop up for them through the year. Experience is key to a successful plan.

If external people need to be engaged to deliver parts of the plan, it is important to have their input in its preparation as well. Similarly, their commitments need to be considered, and their experience when it comes to time and resource requirements is critical for budgeting and scheduling.

Staff may share a high level of connection and values with the team, but, ultimately, it must be the business owners who take responsibility and ownership of the plan's delivery. The team came together based on shared values and a desire to change the current situation. They need to stay connected with the delivery of actions that achieve their goals or the purpose of the business is lost. Not everyone has to take part in the activities, but they do need to provide support, input and involvement in order to retain ownership over the end goal.

ACTION: WORK WITH YOUR TEAM

Discuss roles and responsibilities related to developing and overseeing delivery of the action plan.

- Who has authority over the decisions and expenditure of resources?
- Who will develop the plan and prioritise actions? Who else needs to provide input?
- Who will oversee and manage delivery?
- Who will actually be undertaking the actions in the plan?

What is the purpose of your action plan?

Your action plan may have different functions, but the overall aim is to be useful, efficient and effective when it comes to deciding what to do and when to do it.

The plan will help map out the timing of additional actions to fit around all of the normal business operations and seasonal considerations.

The first function of an action plan is to map out the range of activities and how they relate to the management goals and strategies. A clear connection between activities and outcomes must be demonstrated in order to justify investment.

The second function is to ensure each of the activities is resourced sufficiently, so outcomes can actually be delivered. Resources may influence when results can be delivered and how much can be achieved. This, in turn, influences the timing.

What can be delivered with the resources available within the timeframe?

For example: How many kilometres of fence can be constructed? How many hectares of weeds sprayed? What can be started now, and what needs to wait?

The action plan helps organise the timing of activities to ensure they can be achieved, not only within the timeframe, but with regards to the range of other commitments that exist. It also takes into account the sequence of delivery and the critical dates and external factors that need to be considered.

A documented action plan becomes a communication tool. It extracts a higher level of commitment from the team and other parties who will support its delivery. The plan establishes accountability for the actions and sets expectations about what will be delivered and when. It is also a negotiation tool when engaging external providers, clearly mapping out the schedule and budget for agreement.

The plan is useful for accountability and governance, ensuring expenditure is in line with the purpose of the business. Progress and performance can be assessed against the plan, with resultant reports informing internal decision-making and enabling achievements to be communicated to external stakeholders.

It is helpful to identify how you will use the plan and oversee its implementation. You should also consider the role and interests of other stakeholders.

ACTION: WORK WITH YOUR TEAM

Scope the purpose of the action plan.

- How will the plan be used internally?
- How will the plan be used externally?

ACTION: WRITE THE ACTION PLAN

Heading: Purpose of the Plan
Describe in the opening section of the action plan what the plan will document and how the plan will be used.

Heading: Who it is for
In the introduction, provide a brief description of the key people and their connection to the plan.

CHAPTER 10

What is Logical?

Actions in the action plan need to align with the management goals and strategies. They need to be logical. For every action there is a reaction, which means everything we do has consequences. Action planning attempts to acknowledge and control the intended result of each action taken so that it positively contributes to the overall goals.

Mapping actions against goals increases your confidence that the proposed actions will indeed deliver the intended results. Different types of actions will be considered in the course of this chapter, and address the underlying causes of the impacts they have on the assets. You need to have a strong degree of confidence in agreed actions and review supporting evidence to justify each action proposed. You need to believe that intended outcomes are likely to be achieved.

Actions

Actions are simply things that are done to achieve a result in the short term. Actions need to be effective, appropriate, efficient and, most importantly, they need to contribute to achieving a management goal.

Actions directly implement the management strategies identified earlier. An action plan organises the wide-ranging actions into a logical and coordinated flow. Action plans are sequential steps written up as tasks, which can sometimes be packaged up into projects.

The first step of preparing an action plan is to identify all the key actions for each of the management strategies. Based on the strategies, the actions might already be organised into different categories. Types of action will include:

- On-ground physical work
- Communication
- Administration
- Research
- Planning
- Monitoring
- Reporting
- Partnerships, etc.

The on-ground actions that relate to the environment, natural resources, production systems and infrastructure are generally referred to as BIOPHYSICAL ACTIONS. These actions provide a logical link to improving the state of the physical assets in the management goals.

The other actions, including planning, communication, research, agreements, procedures, etc. are generally referred to as NON-BIOPHYSICAL ACTIONS. These are steps necessary to affect and inform decisions and will logically link to the influence strategies.

It is useful to consider the different action types in order to understand the type of change they effect. If all the actions are non-biophysical, at what point does a physical change in the natural asset occur? Or, if all actions are on-ground, how are you keeping track of progress towards goals?

Milestones encompass major actions or achievements. Five-year milestones were discussed in the management plan. In the action plan, the same concept applies, but in relation to shorter pit stops at the one-year mark or shorter. These milestones are a significant place to stop and review progress.

Outputs are measurable items that result from an activity, such as kilometres of fencing, number of people, plans developed, events attended, etc. Outputs are mini goals that measure progress and help evaluate the approach taken, answering the question: Did the activity achieve what was intended?

Understanding the type of activity identifies appropriate ways in which the result of the activity can be measured. This means you can assess to what degree progress has been made towards the milestone.

ACTION: WORK WITH YOUR TEAM

List actions for each of the strategies.

- Are they biophysical or non-biophysical?
- What are the outputs or measures from the delivery of the action?

ACTION: FARM LOGIC MAP

In the fourth level of the Farm Logic Map, link each of the actions to a management strategy or goal.

Farm logic map structure:

Vision	Growing ethical food that is healthy for families and our environment
State of the Asset 20 Year Goals	Creek system is healthy with good water quality
	Creek is swimmable fish are plentiful — Runoff into creek is clear
Impacts to Assets	Carp — Bank erosion — Sedimentation from paddock erosion
Management Goals 5 Years	20% less carp — 20% less feral pigs — 70% riparian cattle pads repaired — 90% ground cover all areas — 50% gully & by-wash erosion remediated
Management Strategies 5 Years	Carp control — Feral pig control — Fence creek riparian — Stocking rate to increase cover — Pasture on old cultivation — Earth works
Biophysical Actions 1 Year	Carp traps — Shoot, bait feral pigs — 7 km riparian fencing, 2 troughs — Stock days — Cover crop old cultivation — 2 dams by-wash works
Non-biophysical Actions 1 Year	Experts & permits — Pest Mgt Plan — Landcare project — Feed budget

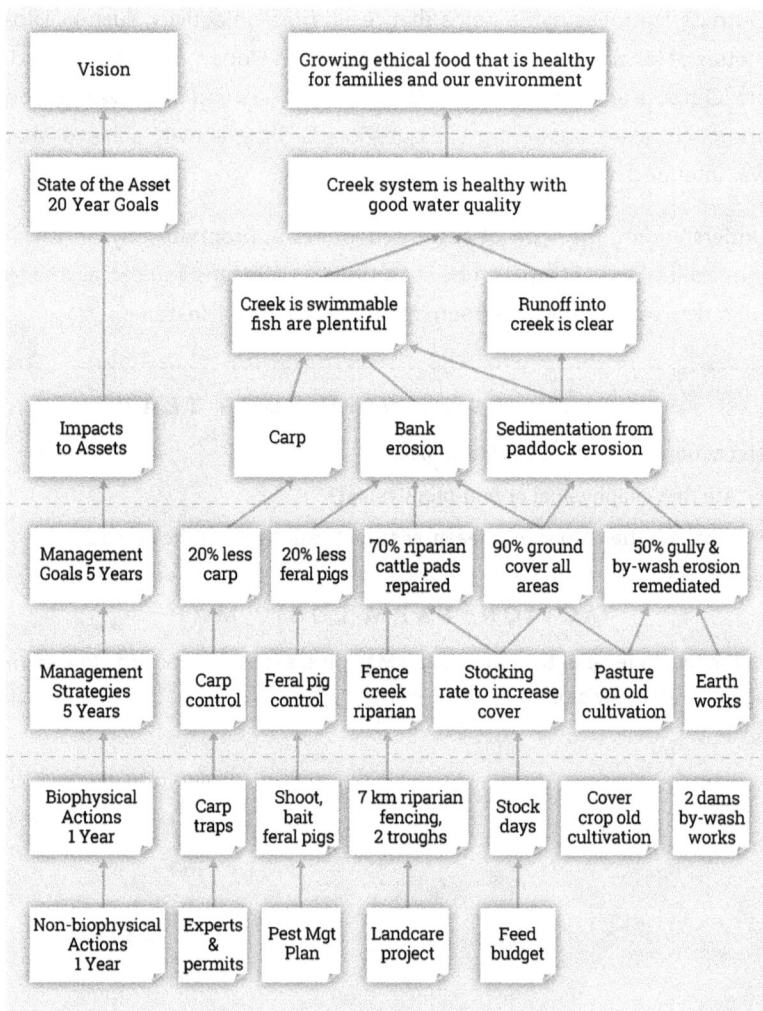

Farm Logic Map 8: Actions (Level 4) Example

Heading: Actions

Asset	Management strategies	Biophysical Actions + output measures	Non-biophysical actions + output measures
Core Asset			
Asset/sub-asset			

Consequences

For every action there is a reaction, or consequence. It is important to understand the consequence of each planned activity and have confidence it will indeed have the desired outcome. Consequences can be intended or unintended. Planning helps reduce the occurrence of unintended outcomes, or seeks to manage them.

Consequences are the result of an action. Threatening processes or impacts are usually the result of unintended consequences. Weeds and pests are a good example, where the action of someone introducing an animal or plant for one particular reason – hunting, food, garden ornamentals, etc. – has caused unforeseen and unintended impacts on other people and assets, such as predation on stock and wildlife, habitat degradation, water quality degradation, pasture encroachment, economic cost of control, etc.

Intended consequences are planned outcomes. The intended consequence of putting in a water trough and riparian fence is to change the behaviour of stock padding along creek banks and mucking in the water, causing erosion and impacting on water quality. The outcome of managing stock access to the creek is restored groundcover and reduced erosion of the creek bank, better water quality, a clean water source for cattle and a separately managed creek paddock.

Sustainability involves foreseeing and managing the compound consequences from past actions and changing the future result for a positive impact on environmental, economic and social assets. Tools such as the Farm Logic Map help you visualise the intended result of each action and the potential consequences for other assets. The process involves asking the question:

If I do this, what will happen?

Every hierarchy level in the logic map is the consequence of the one below. Test the logic with your team.

Not considering the results of actions as consequences may cause you to experience unintended consequences – when it comes to either your own assets or other people's. Considering consequences is a good exercise to ensure that investment in actions is going to lead to the end goal. If you have identified actions, strategies or goals that do not contribute to their long-term goals and vision, they should be further assessed to determine their relevance.

ACTION: WORK WITH YOUR TEAM

Consider the consequences of each of the actions in the action plan.

- If we do this, what will happen?
- Is there anything we need to do differently?

ACTION: FARM LOGIC MAP

Test that each of the actions link to the management strategies and goals in the logic map.

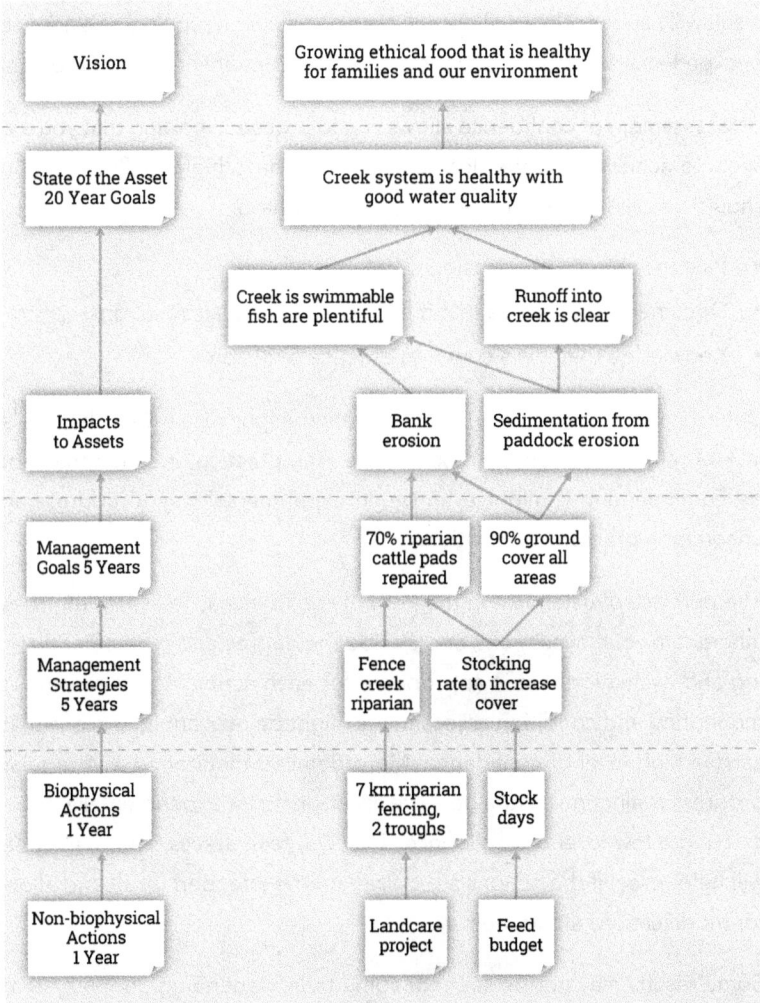

Vision	Growing ethical food that is healthy for families and our environment
State of the Asset 20 Year Goals	Creek system is healthy with good water quality
	Creek is swimmable fish are plentiful / Runoff into creek is clear
Impacts to Assets	Bank erosion / Sedimentation from paddock erosion
Management Goals 5 Years	70% riparian cattle pads repaired / 90% ground cover all areas
Management Strategies 5 Years	Fence creek riparian / Stocking rate to increase cover
Biophysical Actions 1 Year	7 km riparian fencing, 2 troughs / Stock days
Non-biophysical Actions 1 Year	Landcare project / Feed budget

Farm Logic Map 9: Theory of Change (All Levels) Example

Confidence

Once the consequence of each action has been considered, you need to assess the level of CONFIDENCE you have regarding whether the desired result will happen. The level of confidence is based on supporting evidence or experience which has led to the action being determined as appropriate.

An assessment of confidence allows you to proceed knowing that you are likely to achieve the intended results. If you have high confidence, you should be able to demonstrate why. You may have:

- Past experience of an action working locally.
- Documented evidence that it has worked in similar situations.
- Knowledge that it is a common practice or action.

Determining that you have low confidence might reveal that there is a lack of relevant evidence or experience. The practice or action may not be common, and it might even be an experimental way to address an uncommon problem or situation.

The purpose of establishing the level of confidence is to assess the risks inherent in your investment, and decide the degree and type of monitoring and evaluation that is appropriate for each action. Standard output monitoring and condition assessments might be relevant for actions that carry a high level of confidence. More detailed monitoring and regular progress evaluations might be more appropriate for experimental actions carrying a low level of confidence. The 'Do, test, assess, improve' cycle will help reveal if the actions are delivering the intended result and allow for modifications along the way.

Some results may not be seen for some time, depending on the system and rate of change. Relying on the experience of others may be the only basis on which to proceed. The time lag between planting trees and yielding timber or fruit or creating habitat is ten years or more. Making decisions about species, site and design is problematic, as actions can't be assessed for their effectiveness and appropriateness based on results for some time. It is important to consider past experience, locally or in other areas; this helps inform such decisions and reduce the risks involved.

Assessing the level of confidence you have that an action will achieve the desired results is a risk management process. Prior planning prevents poor performance. With consequences and confidence taken into consideration, you can go ahead and map out the tasks knowing you have set up your action plan for success.

ACTION: WORK WITH YOUR TEAM

For each of the actions, consider the level of confidence you have concerning whether they will achieve the desired results.

- What is the level of confidence – high, medium or low?
- What evidence is there to support this assessment?
- What are the mitigation strategies for low-confidence actions?
- What are the monitoring and evaluation considerations for improving future confidence?

ACTION: WRITE THE ACTION PLAN

Heading: Confidence

Actions	Level of confidence (high, medium, low, more info needed)	References, evidence	Mitigation strategies

---

CHAPTER 11

What is Achievable?

Now that the appropriate actions have been identified, hopefully with a high level of confidence that they will succeed across the board, it is time to map out the actions. Resources are finite, so it is necessary to prioritise and set limits in order to see what is achievable within the timeframe.

There are different methods for mapping out the tasks and allocating time and resources to delivering them. Essentially, all approaches need to describe and document:

- What the task is;
- Where it will be delivered or the scope of delivery;
- How long it will take;
- When it will be completed by;
- Who is responsible for carrying out the task and who else is involved;
- What resources are required;
- The cost; and
- Indicators of success.

Even for a small team, these steps are important to ensure time and effort are managed effectively and the job is doable. Undertaking actions that require more resources than are available will have a knock-on impact on other areas. Not everything needs to happen all at once. Planning enables a staged approach over a substantial period of time in order to realise goals in a purposeful way.

What, where, when, who

An action plan is founded on basic information: What will be done, where, when and by whom. Being specific when it comes to each of these elements provides scope and boundaries based on what is achievable and realistic. Mapping them out determines what time and resources need to be allocated.

Actions need to be broken down further into manageable tasks. Be specific so that anyone else reading the plan can easily understand and even implement the plan themselves. What needs to be done? Describe the actions as instructions.

Geographically speaking, where will the activity be happening? Be specific: Where on the property? Where in the paddock? What is the extent or scope of the activity, i.e. how many kilometres or hectares? If the drone were taking a photo, or the activity were drawn on a map, where would it be undertaken and what area would it cover? For management or business tasks, describe what part of the business is involved. Describe what factors inform implementation and put boundaries around what is achievable within the timeframe.

When will the task be completed? This is the first measure of time and is an end milestone. Each task might be sequential and dependent on another task being completed first, such as preparing the ground for planting by August, then planting cotton in September. The other time consideration is how long each task will take to complete, thereby determining when the next task can be started. It also helps to identify bottlenecks or periods of high commitment that need management.

'Who' may refer to the person/s responsible for overseeing the delivery, as well as the person/s actually doing the work. This element of the action plan requires commitment and agreement to the tasks. Ensure discussions take place with external parties early in the planning to avoid disappointment and to factor in any limitations or requirements.

Being specific leads to a higher level of commitment to the tasks. It simplifies complex solutions to complex problems into steps that can be easily understood and followed.

ACTION: WORK WITH YOUR TEAM

Detail the tasks associated with each action, further describing:

- The steps or sequence of tasks.
- Geographic location and the extent or scope of the task.
- The length of time required to undertake the task and the timing for when the task needs to be completed.
- Who oversees tasks and who delivers tasks.

ACTION: WRITE THE ACTION PLAN

An action plan can be presented as a table, a list, or any way that best fits the flow of information. If you use a table, make the headings:

- Action
- Tasks
- Where
- When
- Completed (y/n)
- Who – responsibility
- Who – delivery

ACTION: WRITE THE ACTION PLAN

Heading: Actions

Action	Tasks	Where	When	Who

Resources

Resources refer to a range of things that are required to complete the tasks. Resources can be limiting factors when it comes to what is achievable based on availability or cost. The capacity of an action plan is dependent on resources, which might affect the timing or extent of delivery. Planning resources will help inform budgets and timing and open up opportunities to build current capacity once the full extent of requirements is known.

Resources might include: equipment, materials, software, infrastructure, plans, technology, consumables, staff, consultants, transport, etc. I recommend fully listing the requirements for every task, alongside an estimated budget. The process of identifying what the current capacity is will help prioritise when tasks can occur and identify whether further budgeting is required before proceeding. It also provides a clear understanding of what the shortfall is, based on current available resources and what is required. Tasks may have a wait time before they can be implemented, and additional resources may need to be sought to build capacity.

There are a number of different ways to build capacity to meet the current shortfall. Some actions will be part of normal operations and cause minimal disruption to scheduling and resourcing. However, others may be new projects that require an initial injection of time and resources or ongoing investment.

To bring these actions forward and make them affordable, there is often a range of sources of funding for projects. During the planning, identify what funding is relevant to your situation. After many years of successfully obtaining grants, my biggest recommendation is to apply for grants that align with your business goals and values, as you will be attractive to the funding body and the application will be easier to write. Don't try to change what you want to deliver just because funding is available that doesn't quite fit your goals. Grants are an incentive to bring forward actions, and they are investments in shared outcomes with high public benefit.

To do additional work, you may need to invest in additional people. The way farms operate is changing fast. There are many avenues available through which to engage experienced people. For larger farming enterprises, employing staff may be an option that is feasible and affordable. Otherwise, accessing services might come in the form of engaging consultants or contractors. Many business management and office tasks are now being outsourced using virtual technology. Time is a valuable resource; if there are tasks that others can easily do at a reasonable cost, it is worth the investment to free up time that can be spent in more specialised areas. Time is a significant resource that will be addressed in more detail in the next section.

Forming partnerships might be worth considering if there are other people or businesses who share similar goals. Perhaps they are already achieving goals that you are keen to master. They might specialise in an area, add value to your business, or offer new and different ways of addressing problems. Partnerships may be informal or formal, but should be mutually beneficial. It is helpful to find alignment in values and asset goals, ensuring the scope of the arrangement is agreeable.

Shared arrangements might work for equipment and even staff. Participating in trials, pilots and research is also a good way to access new and emerging technology.

ACTION: WORK WITH YOUR TEAM

For each of the activities and tasks, identify the resources (products or services) needed to complete them. Assess what is currently available, what is needed and strategies to build capacity. Look at:

- Services – People skills, experience, time and cost.
- Products – Consumables, materials, equipment and technology.

Add resources and cost columns to the action plan and list items and their availability. Flag priority resources and tasks that require additional resourcing.

Action	Tasks	Resources	Costs	Priority

Project-it

The list of activities, timeframes and resources may be extensive and overwhelming. Simply putting the heading 'timeframe' in a table doesn't recognise the overlapping demand or delivery challenges in real time. Project-it is my spin on an approach to projecting out the tasks over a calendar.

Project-it mapping considers the milestones and due date for each activity. It attempts to visualise when each of the tasks is due, how they overlap and the time it will take to deliver each task. It also accounts for availability of resources and the sequence of events. It is a hands-on approach that allows tasks to be moved around to consider bottleneck periods, critical events in operations, potential risks and the influence of outside factors.

The easiest approach is to source a roll of whiteboard sheets that you can stick on a wall, or a sheet of Perspex or similar surface. Use Post-it notes to move the tasks about. Set up the board with rows and columns where the overall time period is across the horizontal axis, i.e. a column for each month of the year, and even break it down to indicate the four weeks of each month. The columns should be wide enough to fit a Post-it note. The vertical axis rows are allocated to each project, strategy, person or group of tasks – whatever works for your team.

Dedicate the first row to Critical Events. Here you will map out all of the events that happen throughout the year that are part of normal operations and that impact on the team's ability to undertake additional tasks. These might include planting, harvesting, lambing, preg-testing, etc. They might be internal operations or external operations that impact your ability to engage other people. These events are usually fixed during the year, so use a whiteboard marker to indicate what the event is and when it happens – block out the time period using a line from the start to the finish of the event (whether one day, one week, one month, etc.).

Dedicate the second row to Risks and Influences. These include potential impacts such as wet season floods, holiday periods or staff leave, or anything in your community or industry that will impact on the ability to deliver tasks.

With the limitations now identified, the tasks can be fully projected. Dedicate each row to a project, person or strategy – whatever is most useful for your delivery. *I map according to clients, so I can see what work I have to complete, how long it will take and when it is due. I can manage my own time as well as expectations about my capacity to deliver jobs. I then project my own business management tasks, such as accounting – I even mapped out the publication process for this book. School holidays influence my availability and a couple of annual projects I deliver influence what else I can achieve at certain points of the year.*

For each project, put the final milestone on a Post-it note (hint – peel going left to right; don't pull it up, otherwise it curls and doesn't stick well) and put it on the calendar where it is due to finish. Then, write each of the steps required to deliver the milestone on separate Post-it notes. Put them in sequence and place them on the calendar at the point when they should start. Using whiteboard markers, draw out a line that indicates how long they will take to complete. The next task in the sequence should start after this point. Indicate a buffer period with a wavy line and the critical delivery time with a straight line. You now have a projected sequence of tasks through which to achieve the milestone. The places where you can afford to be late and those where you have a strict deadline are visual. Now you can map out the rest of the activities.

If resource availability is a concern, it might be helpful to use colours. Use green (for go) Post-it notes for the high-priority activities for which you have sufficient resources. Use yellow (for caution) for lower-priority activities that can wait or that are limited by resources. Use pink (for stop) for activities that can't proceed yet or that are dependent on securing external resources, permits, information or other requirements. Use coloured pens to indicate key milestones, progress milestones, reporting requirements and other key factors.

The point of this exercise is to put together a visual overview of all of the things that need to be done, addressing when they can be done and the influencing factors. Set up the calendar year to ensure tasks are achievable at the desired time. If there are delays or unexpected changes, the tasks that are affected can be reallocated and reprioritised, and the Post-its moved accordingly. Having the calendar on a wall makes it visible for the team and makes everyone accountable. It is a great review tool to refer to when discussing progress on a regular basis.

ACTION: WORK WITH YOUR TEAM

Take your team through the project-it planning process for tasks:

- Set up a calendar on a wall with time columns and project rows.
- Identify key influencing events or factors across the year.
- Map the end milestone for each project or action.
- Map each step to achievement of the milestone, accounting for timeframes.
- Identify tasks according to priority and availability of resources.

Project	Jan	Feb	Mar	Apr	May	Jun	Jul	Aug	Sep	Oct	Nov	Dec
Critical events												
Risks/ Influences												
Project 1												

Project plans

A project is different to an action plan. A project is an implementation tool that packages together commitments and actions for a defined group of people, priorities or purpose. It represents a vertical slice of the Farm Logic Map, showing the link between the long-term vision, management goals, strategies and priority actions.

A project plan packages up all the useful information from the strategic level through to the action plan so that it can be communicated and implemented as a unit. It groups together tasks that delivers one or more strategies towards a management goal.

When planning a project, I consider all the components that are usually asked for in funding applications. This represents the minimum information required to communicate the need, intent, value and risks for external investors. Project plans reflect the strategic and action planning of the business, and support the implementation, monitoring and communication of actions and achievements.

When recording a project plan, include the following sections:

About the business – The project plan should open with information about the business, including its vision and purpose (as per the strategic plan). Present details such as contact information, background, area of specialty, area of operation, past achievements.

Project need – Describe the project need relating to the asset. What is the importance or value of the asset and what are the impacts or threatening processes? What is the current gap in management and, therefore, why is there a need for the project? Demonstrate a demand or willingness for the management actions to be supported and adopted, and address why your business is best positioned to address this need. What are relevant industry trends?

Project description – What is the title of the project? Include a short description of what the project aims to achieve. List the key activities and how they link to outcomes (management goals). Describe the approach (management strategies) and why it should succeed.

Activities and milestones – List the key milestones (achievements) and associated activities, timeframes and resources. Justify why these are the best options for addressing the issues and achieving the project objectives. What degree of confidence do you have that these actions will deliver the intended outcomes? Justify this with reference to evidence or experience.

Benefit – Describe the benefit of the project. How will the business, and its owners or employees, benefit? How will the public benefit? (E.g. jobs, repair and protection of assets that share broader community values, flow-on economic, social and environmental benefits.) How does the project solve industry problems and how will stakeholders benefit?

Stakeholders – Who will directly and indirectly benefit from the project? Who supports the project and who is involved with its delivery? What is the contribution from and arrangement with partners?

Budget – What is the business's ability to fund the project? What external funds or resources are required and why? Who will be delivering the services or products? Source relevant quotes. What are the governance arrangements of the business? What is the value for money? Present a cost benefit analysis.

Project management – Who is responsible for overseeing and authorising the project and who is responsible for the delivery of the project? What are the various roles and how will they be filled? How will the project manage the delivery of actions within the specified timeframe and on budget? What previous experience has the business had in managing projects? How will the project be delivered and funded in the future?

Communication strategy – Who are the key audiences and what are the key messages for each audience? How and when will the messages be delivered? How will stakeholders be engaged and what are the performance measures for successful stakeholder consultation?

Monitoring and evaluation – Against the project objectives, what are the key evaluation questions? What will be monitored and when? What are the measures and reporting requirements?

Reporting – What are the internal and external reporting requirements? Who is responsible for delivery of reports and when/how often are they due? How will reports be prepared and who will receive them? How will the project achievements, findings and outcomes be shared?

Risk management – Describe the potential risks, the likelihood of them occurring, their likely impact on project delivery, and the business's response or mitigation strategy. Consider impacts on the timing, budget, capability and situation. Describe any challenges that are anticipated and how you will overcome them. What environmental, social, financial or political conditions might impact on the achievement of outcomes?

Intellectual property – Who owns any intellectual property developed by the project and how will this be managed?

Potential funding sources – If additional funding or resources are required, what are the potential sources? Consider grants, partnerships, investments and loans.

These are the different components that I consistently include in project plans. Even before applying for a grant, I will develop a full, independent project plan. Then, when a grant opportunity arises, I can align and adapt it to the grant criteria. This is more efficient than only writing a plan specific to a grant application when it arises. It avoids the situation of developing projects to fit a funding opportunity, but rather fits the funding to the appropriate elements of the project. Sometimes a project will be broken into stages or sub-projects, depending on the availability and timing of resources.

ACTION: WORK WITH YOUR TEAM

Use each of the items listed above to prepare a project plan when required.

Your Action Plan now provides the business with clear and achievable actions in the short term. They allow you to get on with day-to-day operations and decisions, backed by a high level of confidence that efforts are making progress towards sustainability goals. The actions are planned for the greatest chance of success by having the appropriate allocation of resources, time and people.

In the next part of the book, the decisions made in the strategic, management and action plans will be evaluated to ensure delivery is on track and actually achieving the intended outcomes.

PART 4

VALIDATION

CHAPTER 12

Future Farm Monitoring, Evaluation, Reporting and Improvement Plan

HOW ARE WE GOING?

Simply achieving a goal might be considered success. But perhaps not if there were obstacles and setbacks along the way. What if it cost more than intended, took longer, or the final outcome fell short of expectations or the goal was abandoned altogether? Monitoring, evaluation, reporting and improvement (MERI) activities keep progress on track and assess the overall achievement when it comes to intended outcomes and lessons learnt.

Actions taken to achieve the goals need to be measured and monitored to assess whether they were appropriate, effective and efficient, and whether they achieved the desired impact. The decisions that supported the actions should be validated and evaluated against the overall goals.

Improvement processes should be built into the delivery of all action plans. If there are better, easier, more efficient ways of doing things, you will want to know about it.

Monitoring involves measuring and collecting useful information along the way that helps you demonstrate to what extent actions were delivered and what was achieved.

Evaluation determines if the actions were efficient and effective, and further assesses the overall appropriateness and impact of the approach for achieving the intended outcomes.

Reporting is the documented trail of evidence that helps you evaluate decisions and improve performance. This informs future decisions as you move towards the end goal and helps you communicate with others.

Monitoring, evaluation, reporting and improvement is an approach adopted by the Australian Government for their natural resource management programs. I was introduced and trained in the MERI methodology back in 2007 by Dr Jess Dart at Clear Horizon, a leader in the field of monitoring and evaluation. The underlying program logic process taught by Clear Horizon has brought amazing clarity to my work and the way I help others achieve their goals.

The following chapters cover the processes that aim to validate the decisions you have made. This is the way to integrate evaluation practices with the planning, delivery and review of actions across all areas.

Why do you need a MERI Plan?

A MONITORING, EVALUATION, REPORTING and IMPROVEMENT (MERI) PLAN documents how you will evaluate progress towards your goals and highlights what questions and information will be useful.

You will want to know if your investment of time, money and resources was well spent and that you achieved what you set out to.

You will also want to learn from the process in order to improve actions, experiences and outcomes when it comes to the next phase of delivery. This will also help inform others of your success or lessons.

Focusing on continual improvement is how practices evolve to advance the management and condition of assets and sustainability. Setting evaluation questions at each of the planning stages enables a holistic and comprehensive assessment to be undertaken. Waiting until the end of a delivery period to start the evaluation process means a missed opportunity. It will be a token exercise. In most cases, you will find that the information needed to answer the questions either wasn't collected, isn't appropriate, or can only report on outputs and not outcomes.

The ability to learn and improve throughout delivery avoids the continuation of activities that are not appropriate or effective, and addresses issues as they arise. The goal is to: Plan, do, assess, improve. Knowing what to assess and how to evaluate progress and performance requires planning and consideration. The planning process has already set the business up to easily create your evaluation plan.

A MERI Plan enables you to validate decisions and actions. You can confirm and demonstrate the progress made and have the opportunity to improve on your approach and decisions. Reporting provides an important communication tool for governance, enabling you to justify your investment or that of others. It also informs partners, investors and the wider community about your achievements and demonstrates a commitment to leaving a legacy.

Having evidence to support claims regarding improvement to the state of the assets and investment in mitigation strategies will enable you to attract future investment and partnerships. A lack of evidence lends itself to presumptions about the impact you have made and the value of the investment. This is discouraging for you as well as other interested stakeholders. For all your investment in planning, it is essential you follow through with the ability to validate your decisions and achievement of goals.

ACTION: WORK WITH YOUR TEAM

Discuss why a MERI Plan is important and the benefits of having a pre-set plan.

- What are the benefits of collecting information about progress?
- What are the benefits of setting evaluation questions early?

Who is the plan for?

A MERI Plan has different audiences at different times. It is relevant both within the business and to external parties. It informs monitoring of short-term activities and evaluation of long-term goals. The different parties who have been involved in the development of the plans and their delivery will have an interest in the MERI Plan, which supports the reporting of progress and achievements.

The business owners will be interested in using the MERI Plan to inform governance and decision-making processes. They will be seeking feedback on the efficiency and effectiveness of the actions and value for money in relation to achievements.

Team members will be interested in the extent to which their management goals are being delivered and what that looks like. They will want to know how appropriate the management strategies are and the impact they are having. Are they improving the assets or reducing threatening processes? They will be intrigued to see whether they have been successful in influencing the attitude of others and convincing them to adopt practices or change their opinions.

Both the team and other interested stakeholders will benefit from reviewing the performance of actions and seeing if there are things that could have been improved, changed or accelerated. They will also be interested in your experience, which may affect how they engage and encourage others to take part in the future.

If external communities or stakeholders have impacted on the business, the Farm Logic Map and planning process should identify these pain points. You can use the MERI process to determine evaluation questions. These will relay the result of practices and demonstrate efforts to inform the community.

To what extent could solid evidence influence the attitudes of others?

Interested stakeholders should have input in the plan's development from the start. This will ensure their questions are included and the right information is collected along the way.

ACTION: WORK WITH YOUR TEAM

Identify the target audiences and roles in relation to the MERI Plan.

- Who has ownership of the plan?
- Who has an interest in the plan?
- What level of engagement is appropriate for each person?
- Who is responsible for overseeing delivery of the plan?

Clearly communicate with each audience their intended role and participation in the development of the MERI Plan.

What is the purpose of your MERI Plan?

The purpose of the monitoring, evaluation, reporting and improvement plan is validation. For each of the assets, the MERI Plan seeks to validate the decisions that have been made to realise the desired end state. It is intended as an internal document, but the results and reports form a foundation for external communications.

While the other plans are based on one level of the logic map hierarchy, the MERI Plan is the glue that ties it all together. It tests and validates the THEORY OF CHANGE – that for each decision made and action taken, the consequence has resulted in a desired outcome.

For the actions delivered, it validates the method, extent, expenditure, value and expectations. It sets in place a monitoring program that informs purposeful and meaningful reviews at intervals that help refine the actions for continual improvement.

For the management strategies, it validates the agreed approach. It demonstrates to what extent the actions taken to deliver the strategies have achieved the intended result. It identifies and tests the assumptions and level of confidence in decisions. It measures the accumulated outcomes over time.

The reporting documents the evidence and demonstrates the progress and performance of the team. It sets realistic and meaningful evaluation questions and reporting timeframes. Both the internal and external reporting requirements and expectations are documented.

The reporting provides useful and validated information that communicates achievements and experiences to the team and other stakeholders. It helps to build confidence in the approach, as well as encouraging participation and providing the opportunity to influence attitudes.

The preparation and implementation of the MERI Plan should be a key focus. The MERI Plan is a powerful tool. On its own, it won't deliver any results, but it strengthens all the other plans. A MERI Plan is often required for government grant funding, so it is useful to understand what is involved in preparing and implementing one, and why. However, first and foremost, a MERI Plan must be useful to the business. It should not be prepared for external purposes only. Its worth lies in the fact that it answers key questions and adds value and meaning to the business's implementation program.

ACTION: WORK WITH YOUR TEAM

Discuss the purpose of the MERI Plan.

- How will the plan be used internally?
- How will the plan inform external communications?

Consider the value of monitoring, evaluation, reporting and improvement.

ACTION: WRITE THE MERI PLAN

Heading: Purpose of the Plan
Describe in the opening section of the MERI plan what the plan will document and how the plan will be used.

Heading: Who it is for
In the introduction, provide a brief description of the key people and their connection to the plan.

CHAPTER 13

On the Right Track

The process of developing a MERI Plan helps you stay on track and continually assess your progress and performance. It validates your goals, outcomes, strategies and delivery mechanisms by interrogating their theory of change. It reveals the assumptions you have made and assesses the need to monitor for risk. It helps you to identify the appropriate measures of success and consider how to ask questions about the overall journey and decisions made.

The MERI Plan is the final step you need to take. It builds on all of the existing information, assessments and questioning that has occurred throughout the planning process. It aims to ensure you have the tools to assess performance when it comes to each of the plans and their overall approach.

This chapter will review the decisions made in each of the plans. It brings them together to test the logic behind what you want to achieve and how you go about it. It will look at how you measure and validate success and learn from the experience.

Towards long-term goals

The logic map developed over the three plans now has three main levels and sets out the long-term goals, medium-term management and short-term actions. It is time to bring them all together and test the logic, or theory of change.

Theory of change refers to the story that describes how the actions contribute to the improvement of asset condition until it reaches the desired state.

To review the theory of change, select a pathway leading from each asset to the corresponding management goals, strategies and actions. Test if they align, make sense and tell a cohesive story of change.

For example, from bottom to top: Paige Pastoral aim to progressively repair eroded areas with earthworks on dam by-wash and gullies and seed with improved pasture species (action) to decrease the area of erosion by fifty per cent in five years (management goal). To prevent the occurrence of erosion, an expert will be engaged to provide advice on their pasture and soil management (influence strategy and action). Paige Pastoral expect that these actions will lead to clear water runoff in the streams in twenty years' time, and their soils will be healthy and support optimised pasture health and production (long-term goal).

Or top to bottom: In order to achieve their goal of good stream water quality and optimal production systems, Paige Pastoral will improve the health and condition of their soils. They will achieve this by strategically address- ing areas of erosion around dams and formed gullies and prevent further erosion from occurring based on expert management advice. Paige Pastoral will carry out earthworks and seed bare areas with improved pasture to control and reduce runoff into streams.

For each asset, test the theory of change by starting at twenty years and following the arrows through the levels of the hierarchy.

Is there a logical connection between the three levels for each of the assets that shows cause and effect?

Do all the actions connect to the management level?

Are there things that need to happen before some actions or outcomes are achievable? (For example, securing resources, more research or planning, putting in place agreements.) Ensure these 'foundational' items are listed in the non-biophysical actions.

Consider any assumptions that have been made across the whole logic map, at each level and between levels, and review the actions taken. List the assumptions you have made. For example: Paige Pastoral assumes that soil erosion is causing poor stream water quality and impacting on production. They assume that reducing existing areas of erosion and covering bare areas will minimise runoff to streams. They assume that a different approach to pasture management will prevent erosion from occurring. They assume that experts will offer new information about soils, water and pasture management that will result in changes to the condition of the soil asset. They assume that the cost of advice and control will outweigh the impact to production in the long term. They assume they have the access to the machinery, resources and funds needed to conduct and maintain the required works.

For each assumption, assess the risk of the assumption being incorrect.

Is the risk of not achieving the outcomes high, medium or low?

The next step is to document and/or reference the evidence that supports or refutes the assumptions.

These clarification steps provide assurance that your logic is sound and that your approach will likely have a high degree of success. They aim to validate the design of the overall approach to achieving your goals.

- -

ACTION: WORK WITH YOUR TEAM

Test the theory of change for your Farm Logic Map. Step through each vertical slice of the logic map by telling the story of how each level will be achieved through the implementation of the next level. Discuss the overall assumptions and assumptions at each step, assessing the level of risk and supporting evidence.

ACTION: FARM LOGIC MAP

Use post-it notes to flag assumptions and priority based on risk.

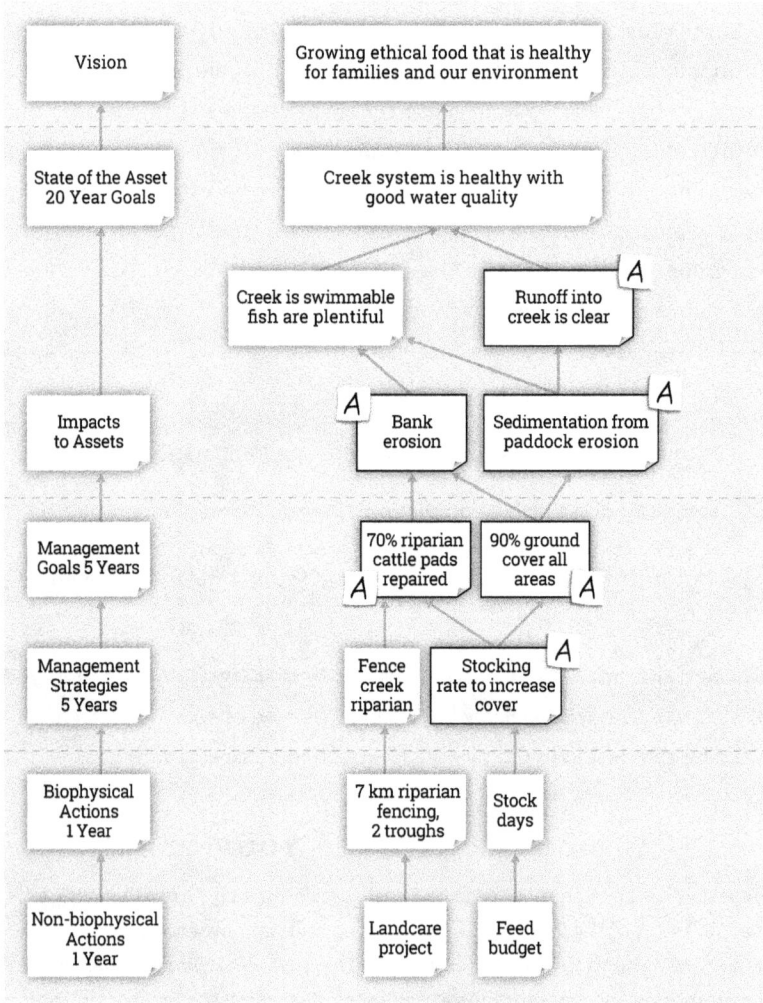

Vision	Growing ethical food that is healthy for families and our environment
State of the Asset 20 Year Goals	Creek system is healthy with good water quality
	Creek is swimmable fish are plentiful / Runoff into creek is clear *A*
Impacts to Assets	*A* Bank erosion / Sedimentation from paddock erosion *A*
Management Goals 5 Years	70% riparian cattle pads repaired *A* / 90% ground cover all areas *A*
Management Strategies 5 Years	Fence creek riparian / Stocking rate to increase cover *A*
Biophysical Actions 1 Year	7 km riparian fencing, 2 troughs / Stock days
Non-biophysical Actions 1 Year	Landcare project / Feed budget

Farm Logic Map 10: Assumptions (All Levels) Example

ACTION: WRITE THE MERI PLAN

Heading: Assumptions

Present the assumptions for the overall logic and for each level of the Farm Logic Map. Document the level of risk associated with the assumption and evidence to support the assumption. The assumption is tested through research and monitoring if there is high risk or lack of information supporting the assumption.

Assumptions	Level of risk (high, medium, low, more info needed)	Supporting evidence	Will the assumption be tested? Y/N	How will it be tested?
Asset Goals 20 Years				
We assume that...				
Management Goals 5 Years				
Actions 1 Year				

Measures of success

The next step when developing a monitoring, evaluation, reporting and improvement plan is to confirm the measures of success and develop a meaningful monitoring system.

There are two types of measures of success. One is directly quantifiable; the other uses an indication. An output is usually a direct measure, such as x number of trees planted or x kilometres of fencing. An outcome is usually measured using indicators that suggest a desired result has been achieved, such as x hectares of increased vegetation, which assumes improved habitat, or x per cent increase of groundcover, which assumes a reduction of sediment runoff. Monitoring is the collection of data and information against the measures in order to report the change that occurs over time.

The goals developed and agreed to in the strategic plan set the long-term measure of success. Each of the asset goals includes a specific measure of the condition of the asset and usually describes an outcome. The desired condition may be a statement and not necessarily directly measurable, such as: healthy soils, swimmable and fishable creek, sustainable beef production. Indicators of success are usually applicable in these situations. Indicators might be: soil cover or organic matter levels, water turbidity, carrying capacity (stock days per hectare).

What are the meaningful measures that demonstrate you have achieved your goals in the long term?

For the management level, the goals usually represent an accumulated sum of outcome measures represented as milestones. These should be directly measurable. For example, the management goal might be: Groundcover is 100 per cent for all grazing areas in five years. Groundcover is measurable; it demonstrates an outcome of management practices and is an indication of soil condition.

What are the meaningful measures that demonstrate you have achieved your management goals?

What are the milestones, e.g. what are the expected measures in five years?

For the action level, each of the activities should have measurable outputs. Outputs are the quantity of an action delivered. For example, x kilometres of fencing, or x staff participating in training. The installation of fencing allows pastures to be effectively managed in order to achieve improved groundcover levels. Participation in training influences knowledge of new practices and attitudes towards adopting them.

What are the meaningful measures that demonstrate activities have been delivered?

The baseline collection of data will help inform the current state of the assets and what degree of change is required to achieve the goals. The change can be broken down to see what is achievable each year, working towards five-year milestones and the desired long-term change.

The next section will address how the monitoring information can be used to answer critical questions to validate the team's decisions.

ACTION: WORK WITH YOUR TEAM

For each goal at the three levels, test and then list the measures of success in a table. Are they output measures and/or indicators of outcomes? Identify duplication and assess the overall requirements and realistic monitoring program. For each of the measures, describe the monitoring requirements, methods and timing.

ACTION: WRITE THE MERI PLAN

Heading: Monitoring

Present the measures of success in a table and describe the associated monitoring program.

Action	Output measure	Outcome indicator	Monitoring method	Timing	Resources
Asset Goals 20 Years					
Management Goals 5 Years					
Actions 1 Year					

CHAPTER 14

How Did You Go?

The final stage in MERI planning is setting evaluation questions. These are questions that interrogate the overall approach as well as the design, processes and impact of your decisions. Evaluation questions enable you to report on success, challenges, lessons and legacy.

Key evaluation questions and sub-evaluation questions will set you up for a successful continual improvement process. Monitoring is important for tracking progress against outputs and outcomes; evaluation seeks to create meaning and value from the information. Validation of the decisions and outcomes is important for transparency and accountability, and for future commitment and adoption of practices. It enables the team to continue to feel a connection with the purpose and vision of the business.

Key evaluation questions seek to validate the overall approach. They address governance and delivery mechanisms and usually relate to levels one and two of the hierarchy logic map. Sub-evaluation questions look more closely at the strategies and actions.

The evaluation questions, monitoring and reporting should help you tell a story about what you delivered, how effective your strategies and actions were, and which areas you can improve in the future. You need to ensure that the monitoring plan is useful and that it's going to add value when it comes to the achievement of your goals. It also needs to reflect your values. Setting evaluation and monitoring expectations during planning allows it to be integrated at every stage, instead of addressed as an after-thought to meet external obligations. A short monitoring and evaluation cycle detects concerns and allows the team to adjust the course of action.

Ultimately, monitoring, evaluation and reporting can validate the legacy of the business and show your overall progress towards sustainability.

This chapter will outline the key components of the MERI Plan and how to write them up with the team.

Establishing key evaluation questions

Evaluation questions focus on what can be learnt. The purpose is to question the impact, effectiveness, efficiency and appropriateness of decisions. Evaluation questions should be open-ended, meaningful and useful, informing future decisions.

Questions should seek to test the assumptions made and align with the values of the team. Imagine being at the end of the timeframe and looking back at what was delivered and what was achieved.

What questions would you want to ask regarding how you went about it?

There are four major areas to address:

Impact – Key evaluation questions aim to demonstrate to what extent the overall investment and delivery approach achieved the intended goals. For example:

- To what extent has investment contributed to the management goals?
- To what extent did education programs lead to the adoption of practices that improved asset condition?
- What, if any, unanticipated positive or negative changes or other outcomes have resulted?

Effectiveness – Key evaluation questions aim to assess how the business delivered its programs. For example:

- To what extent were activities integrated across the delivery programs?

Efficiency – Key evaluation questions look at things like value for money and timeliness. For example:

- How cost-effective was the investment across the programs?
- Were activities supported to achieve delivery within the specified timeframe?
- What other ways could we invest for greater return?

Appropriateness – Key evaluation questions examine approach and management. For example:

- To what degree was good governance applied?
- How effectively did we manage grant investments?
- To what degree were stakeholders engaged?
- To what extent did science inform management strategies?

For each of the key evaluation questions, further sub-evaluation questions will provide more detail, particularly across each of the asset areas. Specifically refer to the relevant programs, strategies, goals and investments. Consider what actually needs to be evaluated in order to answer the key evaluation questions.

ACTION: WORK WITH YOUR TEAM

Develop key evaluation questions that seek to learn about the overall approach and achievement of goals. Develop sub-evaluation goals that support the key evaluation questions and align them with the assets at each level of the hierarchy.

Ask the team to consider the plans as though they have been executed and they are looking back on them, reflecting on their achievements, how they went about things and what they learnt along the way. Imagine the drone zooming right out and consider the overall approach of the team, then zoom right in and consider each of the elements of their delivery:

- Impact
- Effectiveness
- Efficiency
- Appropriateness

List the key evaluation questions. Prepare a table that aligns the key evaluation questions with:

- Sub-evaluation questions for the assets at each hierarchy level
- The measures of success
- The monitoring methods and schedule

ACTION: WRITE THE MERI PLAN

Heading: Evaluation

Present the measures of success in a table and describe the associated monitoring program.

Key Evaluation Questions	Sub-Evaluation Questions	Measure	Monitoring method	Timing	Resources
Impact					
Effectiveness					
Efficiency					
Appropriateness					

Use the project-it calendar to map out the monitoring activities.

Writing up the MERI Plan

A monitoring, evaluation, reporting and improvement plan sets out the continual improvement process for the business. It provides a base from which to review the progress you are making towards your goals and outcomes. And it allows you to learn from and adapt the implementation of strategies.

In the opening section of the MERI Plan, describe what the plan will document and how the plan will be used. Define the timeframe for the plan and the review intervals, for both short-term cycles and long-term observations and assessments. Describe the different target audiences and how the plan is relevant to them.

After the introductory section, the first key section addresses theory of change. This includes the overall logic map developed as part of each step in the planning process. The logic map is important to the evaluation process, showing the cause-and-effect relationships across the different levels. It enables the timeframes, goals, outcomes, strategies and outputs to be clearly articulated.

Document the assumptions made about the overarching logic and the decisions made at each level or between levels. List the assumptions and group them with the assets, indicating the level of risk of each assumption being incorrect – high, medium or low. Reference evidence that supports or refutes each assumption and indicate whether it will be tested.

The next section addresses the key evaluation questions. List the overarching key evaluation questions and break down the sub-evaluation questions relating to each asset area or delivery program. Reference the relevant goals and outcomes.

For each of the sub-evaluation questions, list appropriate measures and indicators for the long-term goals, management goals and outcomes, and action activities and outputs. Detail the appropriate methods for data collection and the schedule for evaluations.

List all the measures identified at each of the three levels in a table. Determine the monitoring requirements for each of the measures. Note what already exists against each of the measures and determine what new evidence is needed. Now the team can determine what should be monitored, how the information should be collected and how often. Further consider how the information will be collated in order to provide meaningful reports on progress.

To keep track of monitoring, make the monitoring activities part of the action plan and project-it schedule. Include the timeframe and resources required to undertake the monitoring activities.

Check that the monitoring will provide relevant and useful information to support the evaluations and identify any gaps. Consider how the information will be reported. It is also useful to draw up a reporting schedule that shows both external reporting expectations and internal reporting requirements. Document the process the team will adopt to review and improve practices based on the report findings.

Further to the reporting schedule, it is useful for the team to outline a communication strategy. Determine who the internal audiences and the external stakeholders are, and what information they will receive, how, why and when. Include these activities in the action plan and allocate resources and time to them.

ACTION: WRITE THE MERI PLAN

Document the key elements of the MERI Plan. Include:

- The agreed theory of change Farm Logic Map
- Evaluation questions
- Assumptions
- Measures
- Monitoring

Include reporting, improvement and communication expectations.

Conclusion

You should now have a full understanding of the steps required to plan and achieve your sustainability goals. Following the Future Farm Blueprint methodology, you will bring a high level of clarity and confidence to the approach you take and decisions you make.

You have the insights and instructions needed to work with the team, so you can find your sweet spot when it comes to enhancing production, protecting the environment, making money, enjoying life and serving your community. You can now:

- Become clear about what you want to achieve and why it is important.
- Fully understand your situation and research the best ways to improve it.
- Build capability in order to implement priority actions.
- Ask questions to learn and improve.

With greater appreciation of what you are trying to achieve and why, you can connect with those around you on a deeper level based on values and understanding. So often, we fall into the trap of only talking about the issues, such as funding, social opinions, legislation and weather, and the focus with our team becomes about putting out fires. Planning and projects serve a short-term purpose and are not often focused on a long-term outcome.

You have the opportunity to influence and lead your team to connect on a deeper level and share a vision for greater sustainability, enabling you to plan clear paths to achieving your goals.

People who plan, achieve.

Some farmers will be seeking a planning and action process that covers all four stages. They may be struggling to achieve their goals and looking for help to gain clarity, knowledge, capability and validation for their approach. They might have new ventures that add value to their operations, and they want to assess how they fit in with their current management and future goals.

Other famers who have been operating for a long time may have lost connection with their vision and their 'why'. A strategic planning process will put them back on track, enabling them to reconnect with their team and focus activities on matters that are important. Having the skills and knowledge to take a team through this process is very rewarding – for them and for you.

I believe many farmers may have struggled because they were so distracted by daily operations that they lost sight of the prize. They simply did not have access to people who could help assess their situation and plan their way to a future with purpose and direction.

The need for people to support each other and work together exists as much today as ever. Somewhere along the line, people will disengage from a poor experience and a farming business with disconnected focus. With a good understanding of the full process, it is easy to see how focusing on only one part can cause a business to flounder.

Simple conversations can bring individuals together to become a functioning team. The connection already exists; it just needs to be identified and shared to form a common bond.

With a newfound understanding of the connectivity between the different planning phases and how to involve people, I hope you can apply what you know and draw on your experiences to bring a deeper level of commitment and control to the team. Assess what you are doing well, where the gaps are and what would benefit you all right now. How can you work with the team to revisit the strategic purpose and validate the delivery?

I believe in sharing knowledge and resources, so we can collectively have an impact. A wide range of supporting resources is available to guide you through the process and writing each of the four plans. Head to the Plan for NRM website for more information: www.planfornrm.com.au.

The most important thing any of us can do is reconnect with our purpose. We each have a role to play and need to commit to making a difference. Thanks for being part of my journey, and I wish you well with yours as you plan, do, review and improve!

Glossary

ACTIONS - Simply things/tasks that are done to achieve a result in the short term and are bound by resources (time, finances, equipment, materials).

ACTION PLAN - Helps to manage the wide range of activities in the short term and focuses on the implementation of the MANAGEMENT STRATEGIES. It organises the timing of activities to ensure they can be achieved, within the timeframe and range of other commitments that exist.

ASSUMPTION - An assumption is something that is accepted as true or certain to happen. In this context, consider the evidence that supports the assumption and the risk of it being incorrect.

BIOPHYSICAL ACTIONS - On-ground actions that relate to the environment, natural resources, production systems and infrastructure.

BUILT ASSETS - Infrastructure, machinery, technology, relating to business operations.

BUSINESS ASSETS - Relate to the business structure, operations, assets, intellectual property, finances, profitability, markets, industry security, employment and access to services.

CONFIDENCE - The degree to which a desired result will happen based on supporting evidence or experience, which has led to the action being determined as appropriate.

CONSEQUENCE - The result of an action, that may be intended/expected or unintended/unexpected and can be either negative or positive.

CORE VALUES - Beliefs, traits or qualities that contribute to an individual's moral compass. Values relate to what people desire in life and include deep personal priorities.

CRITICAL EVENTS - Events or activities that happen throughout the year that are part of normal operations and that impact on the team's ability to undertake additional tasks.

ECONOMIC VALUES - Values associated with the opportunity to generate a fiscal transaction, either directly or indirectly.

ENVIRONMENT - Refers to all things natural, including the physical form, function and system, i.e. anything that lives, breathes or exists as part of a natural process.

ENVIRONMENTAL VALUES - Values placed by people on the environment or particular assets, processes or functions.

EVALUATION - Seeks to create meaning and value from activities undertaken and information collected.

EVALUATION QUESTIONS - Questions that interrogate the overall approach as well as the design, processes and impact of your decisions. The purpose is to question the impact, effectiveness, efficiency and appropriateness of decisions.

FARM - A parcel of land used for the purposes of primary production and processing.

FARM LOGIC MAP - A mind-mapping tool that has the capacity to set future goals and create logical steps to achieve those goals.

FARMER - A person or entity responsible for decision-making and managing a farm. Includes landholders, property owners, managers, corporate entities, etc.

FUTURE FARM BLUEPRINT - The combination of four plans following a methodology that encompasses different aspects of farming, enabling farmers to effectively plan and achieve future sustainability goals.

IMPACT - The extent to which a delivery approach achieved the intended goals.

INFLUENCING FACTORS - Broadly defined as scientific, social, political and economic influences unique to each situation that affect understanding and management.

MANAGEMENT PLAN - Sets five year goals based on knowledge and understanding of the current situation and informs management decisions for high confidence progress towards long-term goals.

MERI PLAN - A monitoring, evaluation, reporting and improvement plan documents how you will evaluate progress towards your goals and highlights what questions and information will be useful.

NATURAL RESOURCES - Broadly speaking, they are landforms, soils, water, plants, animals, sun, microbes, air, etc. Together they contribute to ecosystems, landscapes, biodiverse communities, climate and carbon cycling, etc.

NON-BIOPHYSICAL ACTIONS - Other actions, including planning, communication, education, media, research, agreements, procedures.

OUTCOME - A desired result of an activity, usually measured using indicators, such as x hectares of increased vegetation, which assumes improved habitat.

OUTPUT - A direct measure of an activity, such as x number of trees planted or x kilometres of fencing, x hours of training.

PARTNERSHIPS - Mutually beneficial arrangements that might be formal or informal, to build capacity of the business and add value towards the attainment of goals.

PEOPLE ASSETS - Relate to how people connected to the farm are valued, such as relationships, experiences, knowledge, skills and talents, ambitions, lifestyles and wellbeing. It also includes broader connection that people and communities have to farm assets and management.

PRODUCTION - Primary production or agricultural activities that generate an income, including value adding processes and services.

PROJECT - An implementation tool that packages together commitments and actions for a defined group of people, priorities or purpose.

PROJECT-IT - A tool to project out tasks over a calendar, considering milestones and due dates, resources, sequence of events and overlapping demands and limitations.

PROJECT PLAN - A package of the useful information from the strategic level through to the action plan so that it can be communicated and implemented as a unit. It groups together tasks that delivers one or more strategies towards a management goal.

RESOURCES - The things that are required, or available, to complete tasks, including time, money, staff, equipment, materials, software, infrastructure, plans, technology, consumables, consultants, transport, etc.

SOCIAL VALUES - Values placed on people and their desires for personal fulfilment, and their connection the local and broader community, broadly encompassing wellbeing, contribution, heritage and culture.

STAKEHOLDERS - People or organisations that have an interest or stake in the business and its operations.

STRATEGIC PLAN - A plan that describes what your future farm looks like and what it means to the team and business. It is designed to provide scope for a call to action on matters that are important.

SUSTAINABILITY - Involves foreseeing and managing the compound consequences from past actions and changing the future result for a positive impact on environmental, economic and social assets.

TEAM - The group of people who contribute to or connected with the management and operation of a farm. Includes family, partners, staff, consultants, service providers, etc.

THEORY OF CHANGE - The logic that shows the consequence of a decision made and action taken will result in a desired outcome. It explains the cause-and-effect relationship between actions, management strategies, management goals, asset impacts and goals, and vision.

VISION - A single statement that describes the overall direction of the business and its purpose.

About the Author

Liz Otto is the Founder and Lead Consultant of Plan for NRM, a rural business that helps farmers strategically plan for sustainability.

She has a Bachelor of Applied Science (Natural Systems and Wildlife Management) and is trained in facilitation, project management, program logic and the Monitoring, Evaluation, Reporting and Improvement (MERI) methodology. Liz has eighteen years of professional strategic planning, policy and project management experience in rural areas.

Since the launch of her business in 2012, Liz has worked with over 200 landholders and 50 rural organisations across a range of agricultural industries and specialisations – including beef, sheep, cotton, grains, horticulture, poultry, feedlots, precision technology and machinery, equipment manufacturing, traditional owner land management, renewable energy, pest management and local government.

Although Liz's clients had well thought-out ideas and were implementing practices that aligned with their sustainability ideals, she continued to encounter the same issues with change management on farms. Often projects would be planned in response to immediate issues or opportunities and in isolation from the broader farm objectives. There would be a lack of clarity about those farm objectives across the team, resulting in confusion and overwhelm when integrating new programs or operations. Access to resources and support was often difficult and frustrating. These issues would lead to inefficient and short-term decision cycles.

What frustrated Liz was that all of these issues could have been dealt with by having a plan to guide decisions towards clearly stated goals for the business. This set her on a journey to create a planning system that any farmer can use to plan their future and realise their sustainability ideals. That system has become the backbone of her book *Future Farm Blueprint*, and is the system used to facilitate workshops and prepare strategic and action plans with farmers and other rural organisations.

Liz has been invited to speak as a strategic planning and sustainability expert by the National Rural Women's Coalition as part of their E-Leaders Grow, Innovate and Sustain Program, and the Queensland Ag Show's Next Generation Conference on creative strategic planning for rural organisations.

Many of Liz's clients are leading the adoption of innovation and technology on farms and progressing new industry developments. Using the blueprint method, Liz has leveraged over $5 million of grant funding in five years to support the implementation of strategic projects that clearly demonstrate long-term outcomes. Liz has witnessed first-hand the power of preparing a blueprint to transform a farming business.

About Plan for NRM

Plan for NRM (Natural Resource Management) specialises in strategic planning to help farmers and rural businesses define what sustainability looks like for them and how to go about achieving it.

The business is focused on supporting rural businesses to overcome the frustration and short-sightedness of decision-making and become clear about their long-term objectives.

To help businesses with their planning, a range of resources have been developed and are available from the Plan for NRM website, along with links to other useful resources. These include tips, templates, guides and tools, which are updated regularly. Follow us on social media for the latest release of relevant grants, resources, and industry information and events. Keep in touch at:

www.planfornrm.com.au
facebook.com/PlanforNRM
twitter.com/PlanforNRM

Plan for NRM offers expert facilitation and planning services for farming businesses to prepare their own Future Farm Blueprint for sustainability. Lead Consultant Liz Otto steps clients through a process that takes into account their unique situation and needs, backed by years of experience and industry insight.

Planning packages offer different levels of service based on the four stages of the Blueprint system. Project management and grant writing services are also available to help clients access additional support to deliver priority actions towards their goals.

PLAN
FOR NRM
natural resource management

www.planfornrm.com.au

www.ingramcontent.com/pod-product-compliance
Lightning Source LLC
Chambersburg PA
CBHW070724220326
41598CB00024BA/3289